A PORTRAIT OF HURSLEY

To mark the Golden Jubilee of H.M.Queen Elizabeth II

STAN RAWDON

Published by Stan Rawdon, Keble Cottage, Hursley, Hampshire.

Layout and design by Elizabeth Hallett.
Printed and bound in England by Antony Rowe Limited,
　　　　　　　　　Chippenham, Wilts SN14 6LH.
© 2002 Stan Rawdon.
All rights reserved. No reproduction permitted without prior permission of the publisher.

ISBN   0-9538210-1-3

Other titles by the author:

　　　All Saints' Church, Hursley - a History and Guide. 1993.

　　　Hursley 2000 - A Collection of Memories. 2000.

Front cover: Church Lodge, after a painting by George Frederick Prosser.
Back cover: Typical Hursley Estate chimneys, here on the Old Schoolhouse.
　The Lychgate and All Saints' Church, from a watercolour by G F Prosser, 1859.

Acknowledgements

A book of this kind is not compiled without the help of many people. I wish to acknowledge my thanks to the following for taking the trouble to search for photographs and allowing me to reproduce them in this book.

Thomas Ashbee, Barry Bark, Alan Beusmans, Ben Bone, Revd. Canon Sam Boothman, Roy Bright, Cicely Bull, Eric and Gill Bunney, Sue Buxton, William Clark, Alan Dunk, Dora Ellaby, Tom and Wendy Graham, Michael Hampton, Peter Harris, Sue Howick, Antonia Hawkins, Liz Hallett, David Haskell, John Heath, Rita Hortin, Michael House, Heather and Stephen Ingham, Elizabeth Johnston, Bill Jones, Mary, Viscountess Lifford, Viscount Lifford, Nigel Chamberlayne-Macdonald, Michael McDonnell, Gordon Monger, Tim Moth, Pamela Newton, D.Len.Peach, Claudia Pettifer, Colin Platt, Mary Prendergast, Pamela Pritchard, Pat Pollitt, Joy Ratcliffe, Dolly Richards, Alan Rodbourne, Edward Slater, Dorothy Small, Veronica Smith, Steve Stevenson, Elizabeth Johnston, Anne Syms, Stan Thorne, Dudley Utting, Martin Waldron, Molly Walker. Emma and Murray Weston, Lawrence Wild.
Also to:
IBM UK Laboratories Ltd, Hursley
The Hampshire Chronicle
The Southern Echo
Sky Library of Wadenhoe, Peterborough
Winchester Museums Service.
And an especial thank you to Liz and Mike Hallett for their many hours of computer time.

The parish of Hursley has thrived as a self-contained unit for centuries. The last fifty years have seen a continuation of the many changes that took place during the Second World War. Unfortunately so many photographs, of that time, have been lost. Those included in this book will give future generations an idea of what it was like to live here in years past.

With the generosity of the Hursley Millennium Group and the encouragement of the Parish Council, each household in the Civil Parish of Hursley will be entitled to a free copy of this book to mark the year 2002, the Golden Jubilee of Queen Elizabeth II.

Stan Rawdon, August 2002

Foreword by Mr Geoffrey Squire, OBE,
who bought the Hursley Estate in January 2001

As a newcomer to Hursley village, I feel deeply privileged to be asked to write this foreword.

For many years, the history of Hursley has been inextricably linked to the royal, episcopal and political leadership of Great Britain. It is entirely appropriate therefore that this book has been produced to coincide with the celebrations of the Golden Jubilee of Queen Elizabeth the Second.

Queen Elizabeth enjoys the positions of Head of State, Head of the Church and Head of Parliament.

Hursley's royal connections date back to the Saxon Kings, and continue through the Norman Conquest to the times of Stephen and Matilda.

The Bishops of Winchester owned Hursley Estate for almost a millennium from 637 through to 1559, and they built Merdon Castle as one of six important strongholds spanning southern England. In the 19th century, the preaching and writings of the Reverend John Keble have ensured that Hursley is indelibly recorded in the annals of Church history.

Oliver Cromwell's son, Richard, became Lord Protector in 1658, and in later years two baronets of Hursley from the Heathcote family became Members of Parliament.

Hursley is indeed fortunate to have Stan Rawdon as its unofficial chronicler. This impressive pictorial montage bears witness to an incredible 'labour of love'. It will serve as an enduring record of life in Hursley, to be enjoyed by many generations to come.

When I first moved to Hampshire a few years ago, one of my neighbours told me: "You don't own the land - you just look after it for a while and try to improve it whilst you are here". As the new incumbents of the Hursley Estate, Fiona and I look forward enthusiastically to doing just that!

Geoffrey and Fiona Squire

Golden Jubilee Celebrations, 1st-3rd June 2002

Saturday to Monday: *Flower Festival at All Saints'*
                        Church Tower open
                        Special peal, Yorkshire SurpriseRoyal, rung on the bells
Sunday: *Church service attended by the Bishop of Winchester*
                        Masonic Hall open
Monday: *Village party on the Recreation Ground*
                        Barn Dance in the evening

The street bunting goes up.

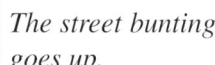

Fiona Squire opens the flower festival in All Saints' Church.

2002, three views of the bells taken when the tower of All Saints' was open during the celebrations for the Golden Jubilee . . .

. . . and two views of the village taken from the tower: right, Lychgate Cottage and above right, The Old Vicarage.

Refreshments after the church service: with cake served by the Bishop's wife, Mrs Lou Scott-Joynt.

The village party gets under way, with Jubilee certificates presented to the children by Fiona Squire. Right: to James Rayner, the youngest inhabitant!

The Women's Group in their Jubilee hats.

The Jubilee village party on the Recreation Ground.

Section Headings

Hursley Park House 15

Views of various Estate properties by Prosser 26

Estate buildings 36

At work on the Estate 49

Merdon Manor 64

Buildings in the main village 68

Further afield in the parish 89

All Saints' Church and its bells 120

Local people -
          The Cooper family 129
          The youngsters 134
          Local people celebrating special occasions 144
          Local people enjoying their leisure 156
          Local people at work 172

Miscellaneous 176

Local transport 183

Three Aerial views 188

Index of places 191

Hursley Park House

D L Peach

Two views of the south front of Hursley Park House, as painted in the 1840s by George Frederick Prosser.

D L Peach

The north-east front of the house as it appeared in 1867.

A similar view in the 1980s, showing the additions built after the Coopers bought the Estate at the beginning of the twentieth century: east and west wings, a domed conservatory and a porte-cochère.

D L Peach

Another of the views painted by G F Prosser, showing a distant view of Hursley Park House from Merdon Castle.

Late nineteenth century view of Merdon Castle ruins and the well.

Views of the former gardens at Hursley Park House.

Gertrude Jekyll gave advice on the choice of plants and the gardens were maintained by fifteen gardeners.

All three pictures: IBM (UK) Laboratories Ltd. Hursley

Peter Harris

The Japanese Sunken Garden painted by Burne-Jones in 1910, is still a pleasant feature, though it looks a little different today.

**Both pictures:
IBM (UK) Laboratories Ltd. Hursley**

Two views of Park House stableyard in the 19th century.
Both pictures by permission of the Winchester Museums Service

Both pictures: IBM (UK) Laboratories Ltd.

Lady Cooper's hospital for officers occupied the second floor of Hursley House during World War One. Lady Cooper is seated in the centre with her daughter, Mrs Wilkie, to her left.
Below: Some of the wounded soldiers with hospital staff.

Both pictures on this page IBM (UK) Laboratories Ltd. Hursley

Above: The American Military Hospital in 1917. This was built in the field south of Standon.

Below: On the arrival of Vickers Supermarine at Hursley Park in December 1940, Lady Cooper welcomed them with this floral tribute to the Spitfire.

Both pictures on this page IBM (UK) Laboratories Ltd. Hursley

The staff of Vickers Supermarine posed outside the main entrance, a picture giving some indication of the large numbers employed at Hursley during World War II.

The Vickers hangar next to the school on Hursley Park road. This was demolished during the 1980s and IBM had a major job to decontaminate the soil.

IBM (UK) Laboratories Ltd. Hursley

IBM (UK) Laboratories Ltd. moved to the site in 1958, initially as a temporary measure. Following the death of Captain Sir George Cooper in 1961 the freehold became available and the company purchased the house and the land within the semicircular access road. Since then many additional purpose-built offices and laboratories have been constructed.

The remainder of the Estate continued to be run by Mr David Wilkie Cooper until it was sold in 1983 to an investment consortium, who held the land until 2001, when it passed into the hands of Mr G. Squire.

1990s - Views showing the development of the site by IBM (UK) Laboratories Ltd.

Both pictures on this page IBM (UK) Laboratories Ltd. Hursley

Over three thousand people are currently employed at Hursley Park.

Views of various Estate properties as painted by G F Prosser in the 1840s for Sir William Heathcote, 5th Bart.

Alan Rodbourne

Home Farm with its yard and some of its workshops.

Alan Rodbourne

Alan Rodbourne

More views of Home Farm and its outbuildings.

Alan Rodbourne

Alan Rodbourne

Four Estate Lodges. Above: Anmery Lodge on the road which leads past Merdon Castle, Below: Merdon Lodge (sometimes known as Castle Lodge), painted in 1841, was demolished in the 1960s.

Alan Rodbourne

Alan Rodbourne

Above: Penfold Lodge was on the edge of Ampfield Wood. Now demolished.
Below: The original Church Lodge, also at one time a gardener's cottage. The girls' school was the long addition behind the lodge, and the whole building has since been converted to become the Parish Hall.

D L Peach

Alan Rodbourne

Above: From Prosser's painting of Winchester Lodge, where the main drive of Park House meets the road to north.
Below: Southampton Lodge at the opposite end of the main drive.

Alan Rodbourne

Alan Rodbourne

Two ex-Estate properties both now in the parish of Ampfield. Knapp Lodge at the top of Knapp Lane has since been renamed Hawkers Lodge.

Brick Kiln Cottage, on the site of the Hursley Estate brickworks, has also been renamed and is now Lower Ratlake.

Alan Rodbourne

Outwood Lodge, Ampfield.   **Alan Rodbourne**

View across Dog Kennel Pond to Keeper's Lodge.
Alan Rodbourne

Alan Rodbourne

Two views of Merdon Castle ruins.

Alan Rodbourne

The Vicarage, painted in 1859, and All Saints' Church.

1859, the lychgate, showing the old fence paling. **Alan Rodbourne**

The Swiss Cottage stood in the Fernery in the Estate grounds near Merdon, but has now been demolished. **Alan Rodbourne**

Estate Buildings - more recent pictures

Home Farmhouse, 2000.

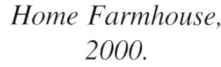

The bell.

Home Farm buildings, 2000.

The carpenters' shop, Home Farm, 1960s.

Home Farm sawmill with Sunlight Cottages in the background, 1960s.

Selina, Lady Heathcote, wrote in her diary on 28th November 1842: 'Went to see new machinery at the farm, which is now nearly completed, consisting of threshing, winnowing and turnip cutting machines, oat crusher, chaff cutter, flour and barley mill, bone mill and sawing and turning apparatus, all worked by steam.'

The freshwater pumping plant at Home Farm. The pump was situated over the well and pumped the water to a reservoir at Violet Hill and another at Farley. The system was dismantled in the late 1950s.

This had replaced an older system whereby water had been gravity-fed from a reservoir at Ladwell.

The pump over the actual well.

Note the spun-glass windows.

The House was served by a refrigeration plant which was sited in the south-west corner of the stable block. This, too, was dismantled in the late 1950s.

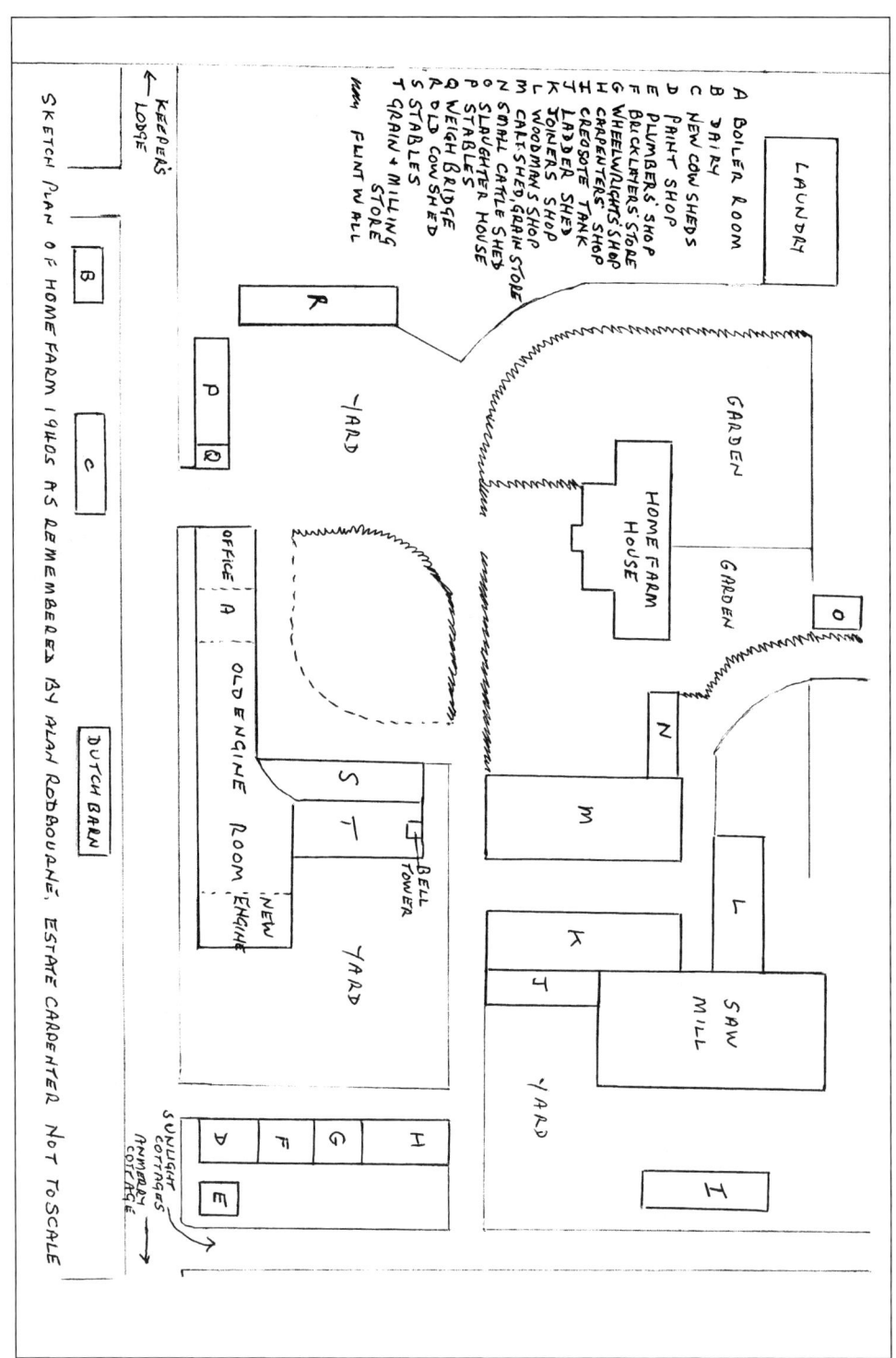

The Estate Dairy, under construction in 1909 and later after completion. It has now been demolished.

Former Estate Office (left) and Home Farm Lodge (right), both demolished in the 1960s.

The Estate Office, previously the Estate Laundry. 1980.

Sunlight, 1990.

Violet Hill Cottage, 1996.

Southampton Lodge in 1925, with Mr and Mrs Lewington. He was the Estate's head gardener.

The present Church Lodge in 1999.

Above: Merdon Castle Lodge in the 19th century.

Above: Anmery Lodge in the 1970s.

Above: An aerial view of the nearby Anmery Cottage, mid 20th century. Below in 2002.

Winchester Lodge, formerly Bowling Green Cottage, demolished in 1960. IBM arrived in 1958 and put up their sign as shown in the photo, causing great amusement to American visitors who had expected the laboratories to be rather larger than this cottage!

The old gardener's cottage in 1999, now part of the Parish Hall.

Two views of the old Church Lodge (previously a gardener's cottage) with the girls' school adjoining the rear.

At work on the Estate

Two pictures taken on the Hursley Estate in the 1890s. Above: two Fowler 8hp ploughing engines, nos. 2860 and 3677.

Two Fowler horizontal-shaft traction engines, nos. 2733 and 2734, sold by the Estate in October 1892.

At Home Farm about 1880-90, some of the Estate maintenance workers, Mr Bradley in the centre wearing the bowler hat.

Hursley Estate workers circa 1900. Back row L to R: Cole, Cole, Bullock; Front row L to R: Edwards, Haskell, Balsom, Eagle, Woller.

Building the Estate dairy in 1909.

About 1910, the creosote tank at Home Farm sawmills, used to impregnate timber. Left is Fred Dewey and right is Stephen Whitbread.

Above: Fowler-Goode ploughing engine. Driver: Fred Weight, with Bill Jerram to his left, 1920s, possibly taken at Enmill Farm where the machines were stored.

Driver Thomas Salter with Bill Jerram on the left.
One of L H King of Pitt's ploughing engines. 1920s.

A group of Estate maintenance workers in the 1920s.

Mr Tarrant, the Estate carpenter is on the left in this photo.

1920s, William Clark with his hands on hips.

Thomas Salter, tractor driver with Thomas Taylor on the binder, 1920s.

Archibald Savage, Estate clerk of works in the 1920s.

Estate woodmen early in the twentieth century.

A group of workmen on and beside an early lorry. Possibly taken during the construction of the reservoir at Violet Hill, pre-1910.

William Bark, Estate gamekeeper, with his wife, Mary, and son, William, 1920s.

William Bark, outside his home, Church Lodge, circa 1940.

Three Estate painters, 1930; L to R: Elliott Collins (foreman) of Knapp Lodge, Harry Misslebrook of Ratlake and Frank Haskell of Knapp.

Haymaking in the 1930s.

Harvest home.

Milking time.

Home Farm cowsheds in the 1930s.

William Clark was the driver of this Fowler Compound Traction Engine in 1935.

Frederick Hyde, Albert Sainsbury and Edward Mildenhall making silage at Berrydown Farm in 1939.

William Clark at a ploughing match, 1951.

Using a 1918 Marshall threshing machine. This photo was taken at Crabwood in 1975, with C H Waldron on the extreme right.

Deer shoot, 1930s, with Frank Fielder third from the right in the back row.

Counting the total after a hare shoot at Standon Farm in the 1950s.

Rabbit shoot 1971; L to R: George Badkin, Chris Bolton, Walter Carter and George Pierce.

Lunchbreak during a hare shoot. Left to right: ?; Les Fielder; Frank Fielder (head keeper); Alf Burrows; Les Summers; Cecil Summers.

Merdon Manor
By permission of the Winchester Museums Service

A 19th century view of Merdon Farm, which was to become Merdon Manor.

Merdon Manor - with alterations in progress in 1983.

The old barn at Merdon Manor.

Merdon Manor after alterations in 1983.

The late Lady Cooper used this converted shepherd's hut as a painting studio. Below: Her work was displayed in this studio at the Manor.

Merdon Cottages.

Buildings in the main village

Two views of the village centre from the church tower,
Above: towards the King's Head and Collins Lane, 1980s.
Below: towards Meredon Close, 1989.

Ernest Wild outside his cottage, No. 17. This lay just on the Winchester side of the IBM drive at the north end of the village, and was demolished in the 1960s.

Hollyhock Cottage, 1999.

1975, Brian Taylor in his shop at North End, above with Percy Caton, right with Jan Rodbourne.

A view of No. 33, showing the thatched wellhouse in the garden next door. A spark from a traction engine stopping for water ignited the thatch of the cottages alongside, burning them to the ground. Tudor Cottages were subsequently built to replace them.

Sussex Garage in 1956.

The car showroom built by John Sussex when he took over the Hursley Garage. When this photograph was taken in 1999 it had become an antique shop, but now this too has closed down.

The King's Head in the late nineteenth century showing the old stable block.

Hursley Garage 1950s, with the petrol pumps sited right outside the pub door.

Collins Lane, 1999.

Below: the Granary behind the King's Head, dismantled in the 1950s.

Dora, Ivy and Elsie Bunney outside 58 Collins Lane, about 1938.

**Hampshire Record Office and Hants Field Society.
Ref. 65m89/2130/23**

The Square, 1986, formerly the Union Workhouse.

The Old Court House, also 1986.

The village shop and forge, 1919.

Re-roofing Number 78 in 1963.

Almost the same view of the village centre. Above in the 1880s, before the days of tarmacadam, (note the old cottages which Mr Joseph Baxendale replaced with the present mock-Tudor row). Below in the 1930s, with more people than vehicles!

Peter, youngest grandson of G H Jones outside No. 78 in 1929. The notice is advertising recruitment for the Royal Navy and Royal Marines!

The rear of No. 95A in the 1920s.

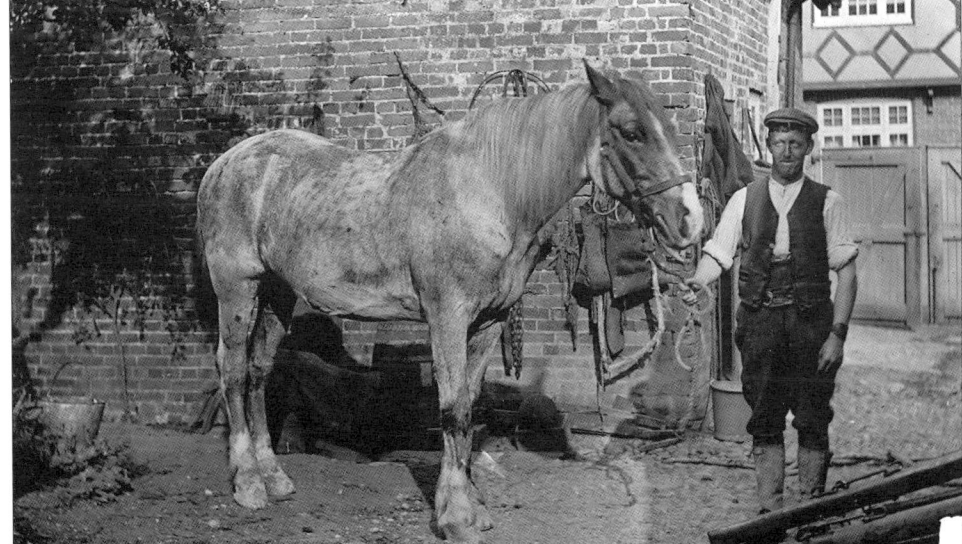

Hursley is prone to flooding in very wet weather. Here a flash flood near the Dolphin in 1979.

Number 95 in 1989, just before being divided into two properties.

Carriages by the forge, early twentieth century.

The forge in 1906.

*William Wild, saddler, outside his shop, No. 97, in the 1880s.
Later a greengrocery, these premises finally closed in the 1960s.*

*The Saddlery circa 1910,
with Ernest Wild standing behind the pony and his son Walter in the trap.*

Ernest B Wild (centre, with his daughter, Clara) outside the Saddlery in about 1914. The lad on the right is his son, Harry.

The Old Saddlery in 2002. The medieval hinged shopcounter can still be seen, painted white, below the left-hand window.

Number 98a, Keble Cottage, in 1940 and in 1999.

Southern view of the village in 1969.

Archibald Savage, landlord of the Dolphin Inn in the late 1920s.

An aerial view taken from Dolphin Field in 1985.

Hursley Bakery in the 1980s with Antonia Hawkins, Joanna Morgan and Sue Howick.

Pelican Court 1986.

Above: The market gardens on the glebe lands, photographed after being left uncultivated prior to the start of construction work on Meredun Close, which now occupies the site. Below: Building work in progress, 1987.

Number 100, Hursley in 1999. The house dates from the 1950s but was built using one of the commercial designs of Sir Edwin Lutyens.

The schoolmaster's house early in the twentieth century, with children gardening in the foreground.

*The former police house, above in 1999,
below in 2002 following extensive alterations.*

Southend House, behind its high flint wall.

Two notable buildings of old Hursley, both now gone and their place taken by new development.

The Pelican Inn which became the Pelican Farm, with left: a view of its garden. Now the site of Pelican Court.

Further afield in the Parish

By permission of the Winchester Museums Service

Standon House, on the corner of the lane leading to Merdon, pictured in the nineteenth century.

Today the house has been rendered and painted cream, losing the decorative stonework around each window. It has been divided into four flats.

Standon Farmhouse, on the junction with the lane leading to Sparsholt, as it was in the 1920s.

At Standon there was once a fair-sized hamlet. This old cottage, photographed in 1978 remains, but others nearby have been demolished.

Above: a distant view of South Lynch in the 1980s. Left: the house in 2000.

South Lynch Cottages at the same period.

A view of Pitt's Church of the Good Shepherd and Church Cottage in 1870.

Pitt's school-cum-chapel three years earlier in 1867.

A similar view in 2002.

Pitt.

Church Cottage, beside the Church of the Good Shepherd. One room was once used as a school.

Enmill Lane.

Three views taken in the snow, January 1985.

Oddicombe and Wayside Cottages.

1987, view from the roof of Church Cottage, looking east.

An aerial view of the hamlet of Pitt in 1988.

Pitt was known in the fourteenth century as 'Putte'.

A terrifying series of arson attacks took place in Pitt between 1988 and 1993. After four thatched cottages had been set alight, some more than once, a thatched garage, at least seven barns with straw bales and haystacks, a local farmworker was eventually brought to trial on charges of starting nineteen fires. Six of these convictions were later quashed for lack of evidence but he spent some years in jail.

White Cottage (above and below) was one of the cottages very severely damaged by fire in April 1991 and its garage in May 1993. Oddicombe Cottage and the neighbouring Wayside Cottage were each set alight, one in April 1991, the other the following February.

Unbelievably, (above and below) White Cottage having taken a year to repair, caught fire again in 1996, this time caused by sparks from a wood-burning stove.

*Above: Pitt Vale Farm, 2002
and below: the farm outbuildings, now converted into homes.*

There were originally two cottages at the Pound, seen here before one was demolished around 1960.

The remaining 16th century Pound Cottage still stands, photographed below in the 1940s.

Pound Cottage, front and rear, showing the 1993 extension.

The road junction at the Pound in 1998.

Ladwell

One of the remaining thatched cottages at Ladwell, No. 137, taken in 2002. The cottage dates from 1775 and was extended in the 19th century.

Red House on Ladwell Hill. It was here that Samuel Heathcote lived until his death in 1797, as did the Revd. John Keble when he was the curate for a short time in 1825. The house was extended c. 1875. In the grounds is a well reputed to be the holy well (Our Lady's Well) which gave the hamlet its name. Here in the 1970s.

Field House

Field House, dating from the early sixteenth century: left: before and right: after being extended in 1900.

1904.

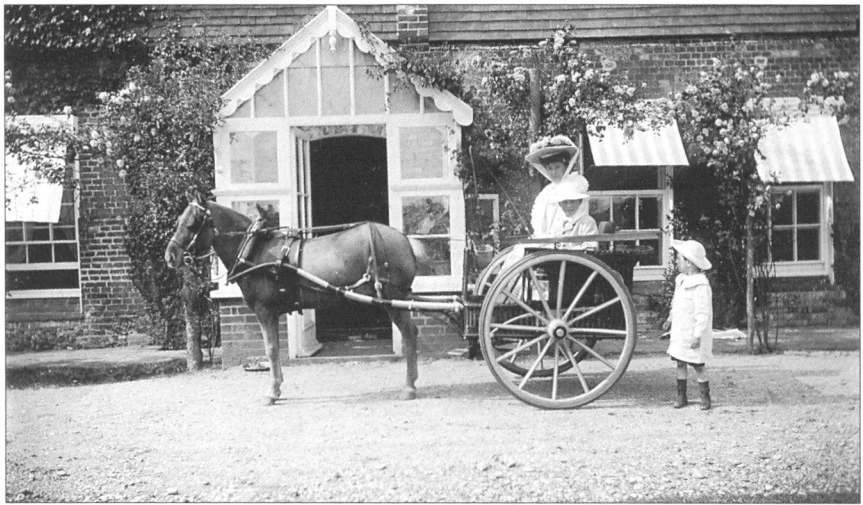

Members of the Hewitt family at Field House, 1904.

The main road through Ladwell in the days before the motor car!

Views of the Remount Camp at Longmore during World War One.

Cranbury Park.

Berrydown Farm and its outbuildings, 2000.

Berrydown barn, and its interior, 2000.

Two more barns - these are in Bunstead Lane. Both were once part of Parsonage Farm and the lower one has been converted into a home.

Shawlands in the 1980s.

A distant view of Shawlands Cottages in 2002.

Two views of Parsonage Farm in 1982.

As seen from Ladwell.

Renovation of Parsonage Farm in 1978.   Southern Echo

1980, the 12 foot treadwheel and well incorporated into the sitting room.

Views of Silkstead Farm in 1913.

Silkstead Farm and pond in 1913.

Down Farm, 1990s.

*'Dummers', 1904, when it was the last house on the Hursley Estate, bordering Braishfield.
Left to right: Mary Goulding, Eva Williams (later Eva Fielder) Fanny Williams (née Goulding) and Jesse Goulding.*

Dummers as it is today - part of Pucknall House. Note the gap in the roof ridge where the tall chimney used to be.

The horse monument at Farley Mount, from a painting by G F Prosser.

The monument at Farley Mount and the story behind it.

*Twelfth century Church of St John, Farley Chamberlayne.
Below: in 2002.*

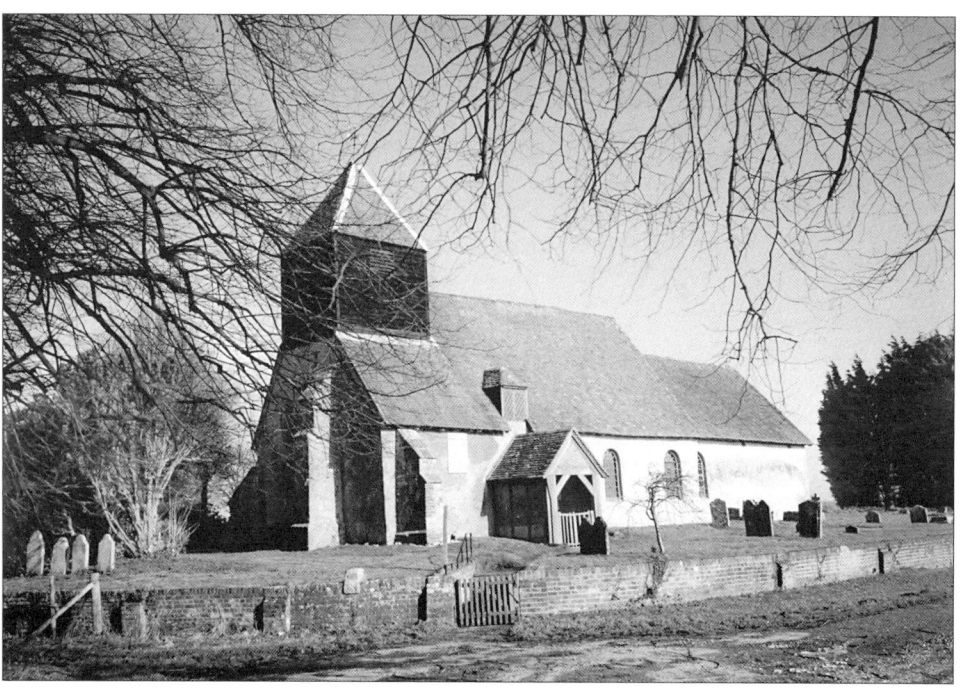

Two views of the interior St John's Church after restoration by Sir George Cooper in 1910.

This font in St John's Church commemorates the Millennium walk from Farley Chamberlayne to Canterbury. It was consecrated by the Bishop of Winchester on Advent Sunday, 2000.

Farley Chamberlayne Farm, above in 1940 and below an aerial view in 1962.

Farley Semaphore, built 1830-31 as part of the semaphore line from London to Plymouth. The line was never completed because of the introduction of electric telegraphy. Later in the 19th century and until 1911 it was Telegraph House Boys' and Girls' School, Farley.

The Old Schoolhouse at Oaklands, Farley as it is today. Compare this with the photographs taken in 1953 on page 133.

All Saints' Church and its Bells

Hursley's fourteenth century church tower, from a sketch about 1845 by Maria Wilson, née Trench, Lady Heathcote's niec. She was the wife of Keble's curate Robert Wilson, who became the first incumbent of Ampfield.

The barn in which the Revd. John Keble held services whilst All Saints' was being rebuilt during 1847/8. Taken from a painting by Caroline Elizabeth Heathcote, 1849.

Alan Rodbourne

Keble's drawing room in the Vicarage.

The Revd. John Keble, Vicar of Hursley 1835-1866.

View of the Vicarage across the churchyard in 1867.

Removal of the spire in 1960 by Claspers, steeplejacks of Ringwood.

The church and its churchyard c. 1900, as it was before the graves were levelled.

The above postcard, which commemorates the recasting of the tenor bell in 1923, was actually posted in 1943.

A social gathering on the Vicarage lawn in about 1910. Extreme left: Archibald Savage who was Estate clerk of works, later, in the 1920s, landlord of the Dolphin Inn. Standing is the Revd. Thomas Pughe.

Removal of the trees in the churchyard in 1952. It is said that these had been planted by Richard Cromwell.

Four of the Victorian windows at All Saints', depicting Adam, Noah, Abraham and Melchizedek.

The Heathcote Mausoleum, interior and exterior.

The weathercock on All Saints' Church, 2002.

All Saints' Choir early in the 20th century.

All Saints' Choir 1961.
Standing: Roy Hampton, Mr Ronald, Philip Horn, Percy Harris, Ann Griffin, Mr & Mrs Ashford, Revd. H Llewelyn, John Horn, Dorothy Wild, Colin Eades, Carol Gent, Peter Horn, David Horn, Sir John Alleyne. Seated: Cicely Fielder, Winifred Randall, Rosina Wild, Pauline & Denise Kew.

All Saints' bellringers in 1960 include: Bill Eades, Colin Eades, Mr Compton, Mr and Mrs Hopkins, Revd. and Mrs Llewelyn, Anne Holford, Cicely Fielder, Denise Kew, Rosina Wild, Pauline Kew, Carol Gent.

Hampshire Chronicle

The bellringers of 1989, L to R: Ian McCallion, Martin Waldron, Jesse Kippen, Anthony Smith, Phillip Belgeonne, Bruce Purvis, Brian Lovelock, Charles Kippen, John Croft and Andrew Craddock.

Above: The framework for the two additional bells for All Saints', 1989 (making a total of ten), with L to R: Bruce Purvis, Bill Barnes, Tony Smith and David Burge. Below: The two new treble bells, which incorporated metal from two small bells donated by St Luke's, Stanmore.

Local People: the Cooper family

The first Sir George with Lady Cooper, circa 1938.

1938, Sir George and Lady Cooper's golden wedding, with Left: the oldest tenant, Fred Jones, postmaster and Right: Elliott Collins, printer, the oldest estate worker.
Hampshire Chronicle

Tenants celebrating the golden wedding of Sir George and Lady Cooper, 1938.

Sir George and Lady Cooper in 1924 with Alan Hewitt of Field House, later the 8th Viscount Lifford.

George W Hewitt of Field House, father of Alan and Dennis.

Denis G W Hewitt VC of the 14th Hampshire Regiment, killed in action on 31st July 1917.

Hampshire Chronicle

Sir George Cooper's funeral cortege leaving All Saints', 1940, Sidney Williams leading estate horses.

Captain Sir George Cooper during the 1950s, above: in the grounds of Merdon Manor, below: at Farley Chamberlayne.

Captain Sir George Cooper at Farley Flower Show in the 1950s outside the School House. (Also in the picture, L to R: Mrs Mary Boothman, Revd. [later Canon] Sam Boothman [standing], Fred Chapman, Tom Ross, Revd. Canon George Uppington, ?, Mrs Lucy Chapman, Mrs Elsie Graham.)

Presenting the cups on the same occasion.

Local People: the youngsters

Two school groups: Above: in 1912 including Douglas Jones centre back row and Bertha Savage front row 3rd from the right.

Below: - the infants in 1933, with William Clark back row extreme right.

Hursley School senior class, probably 1933.

Below - Mrs Dorothy Dickman's class in 1936.

Hursley School Choir in 1966 with headteacher, Mrs E M Warr.

Members of the Merdon Lodge of Freemasons look on as Cliff Lassam and Zoe Tai inaugurate one of two drinking fountains at John Keble Primary School, Jan 2002.

Mayday was celebrated in the village for many years. Above: a view in 1931; Below: Lady Cooper presenting Irene Adams, with her May Queen's brooch.

More of the annual mayday celebrations later in the 1930s.

Hursley Girl Guides, circa 1916.

Hursley Brownies in 1934.

The scouts guarding their bonfire at Farley Mount, possibly to mark the coronation of King George VI in 1937.

Hursley Scout Troop outside Catways Hut in 1938.

The Scouts with their leader, Arthur Bunney, camping in the field behind Home Close.

Hursley Scout Troop in 1946.

1st Hursley Troop - Boy Scouts, July 1949.

David Faithfull	Keith Potter	Patrick Udell	Robert Lloyd
Peter Potter	David Jones	Michael Blandford	Eric Bunney
John Turley	Colin Eades	Arthur H Bunney	Reg Richards	David Giles
		Scoutmaster	Asst. Scoutmaster	
John Pike	John Coak	William Blackford	Ian Jones	David Pike

Camping on Hayling Island in 1951.

1st Hursley Scouts' Gang Show 1954 at King Alfred's College.
L to R: ? Smith, Roger Elkins, ? David Hewett, Richard Tear, Barry Bark, (sitting) Victor Carter, Gary Rainsford, ? the bear, ?, Brent Heath, Aubrey Jones, Bernard Lea, ? Smith.

Scout camp at Merdon in 1954.

Scout camp on the Isle of Wight, 1955.
L to R back row: Barry Bark, Gary Windebank, David Ryley, Alan Jeffery, Gordon Stainer, Fred Elkins (scout master), John White, Colin Eades, Tony Cottrell. L to R middle row: Kenneth White, Tony Southwell, John Dickinson, David Cottrell, George Windebank. L to R front row: Scott ?, Brent Heath, Aubrey Jones.

Local people celebrating special occasions

Festival of Britain carnival, 1951.

Mac Axford leading the horse and Charles Rodbourne driving the tractor.

More 1951 carnival floats: above - representing the Women's Institute, and bottom - the Tennis Club. Centre: members of the tennis club float ready for the procession to start.

Three photographs of the 1953 pageant which celebrated Queen Elizabeth II's coronation. Mrs Warren was Queen Victoria and was attended by Percy Harris.

Coronation Day 1953 was also celebrated at Farley at the school house.

Marking the centenary of John Keble's death, 1966.

Hampshire Chronicle

1977 The Queen's Silver Jubilee.

There was a party for the children in the Parish Hall.

Charlie George (Southampton FC) and Jan Rodbourne presenting commemorative coins to the children on the occasion of the marriage of Prince Charles and Lady Diana Spencer, 1981.

A village party was organised for the occasion by Carol McDonnell, Philippa Syms, Sue Olden, Jan Rodbourne and Cicely Bull.

Celebrating the 50th anniversary of VE Day in 1995.

2000 AD.

Millennium celebrations in Hursley.

Stan Rawdon selling his millennium book, 'Hursley 2000', at IBM's Open Day.

The Hursley Millennium Tapestry, designed and co-ordinated by Dora Ellaby, here being shown to the Mayor of Winchester, Cllr. Georgina Busher, the May Queen, Georgina Rees, Parish Council representative, Rossi Heath and Chairman of the millennium group, Hazel Corney on the occasion of its unveiling. September 2000.

Sheila Rawdon, Mary Freemantle and Dora Ellaby with the tapestry in the Parish Hall.

Millennium oaks. Children planting oak saplings grown from acorns in school to commemorate the millennium.

Millennium Christmas tree - with mulled wine served after the Christingle service.

John Defty of Keble Primary School receiving the first Millennium Prize for history from Stan Rawdon.

Local People enjoying their Leisure

The Hursley Hunt. Above: at South Lynch House with Sir John Alleyne in the black jacket, 1970s. Below: at Jermyns House, Ampfield.

Members of the Tennis Club in 1951. Standing: ? ; Colin Eades; Seated: Mr Ashford; ?; ?; Caroline Ford; Mrs Ashford; Seated on the ground: Hazel Richards and Alison Kew.

Eva Fielder with young supporters of the Hursley Cricket Club, 1975.

Hursley Cricket Team 1950s.
Back row L/R: Alan Jeffery, Ernest Pittard, George Bavington, William Bulpitt, Michael Hampton, ? Nichol, Alec Kew, William Fielder (umpire), Frederick Bunn
Front row: Peter Hobbs, Ronald Churcher, Philip Pratt, George Collins, Frederick Clothier, Mrs Clothier (scorer).

Hursley Cricket Team 1960.
Back row:L/R: William Merritt, Alan Rodbourne, Alan Permain, Alan Jeffery, Peter Hobbs
Front row:Brian Gillingham, Frederick Down, William Fielder, Leonard Lockhart, George Collins, Frank Cottrell.

Hursley Bowling Club. A game of bowls on the recreation ground in the 1930s, using Richard Cromwell's woods. Below: George Jones looks on as Ernest Wild decides the winner. Standing to the left is T Ashton, agent for the Estate, and to the right: A H Dunk, clerk of works.

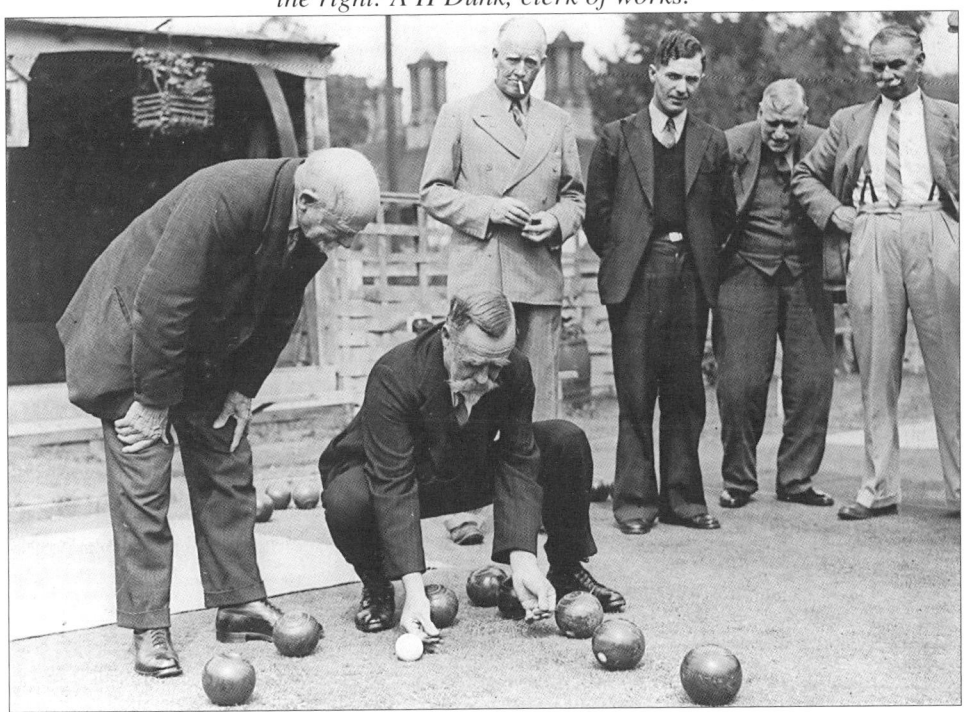

Two photos of the W.I. folk dancing group.
Below, 1919: Standing - Maggie Street, M Cooper; Back row seated - G Pinnick, A Whitmarsh, Bertha Savage, W Hunt; Front - Hilda Street, M Hunt, H Andrews.

An evening at the King's Head. R to L includes: Bert Messam, Reg Gardiner, Charlie Bunney, Jock Delgarno, Arthur Bunney, Mr Collins the landlord (seated), Mrs Collins, Ken Bright, Reg Freemantle, Alec Kew jnr., Louis Bright.

Members of the King's Head darts team 1955/6, which won the 'Airborne League' that year. The group includes L to R: standing - Frank Randall (landlord), Alec Kew, Alfie Bond, Bert Messam, Alan Rodbourne, John Coak, Alf Burrows; seated - Vic Carter, Frank Cottrell.

Two photos of Hursley Women's Group Christmas Party, 2001.

Left: Antonia Hawkins, Ann Beusmans, Christina Sermon, Jan Rodbourne, Gill Edwards.

Right: Gill Edwards, Cicely Bull, Anne Syms and Gwyn Dickman.

All Saints' Christmas party 2001.

Left: Gill Edwards, Cicely Bull, Revd. Roger Edwards, Pam Newton, Carol McDonnell, with Mick Wright in the background.

Hursley teenagers, 1960s. The group includes Steve Beasley, Garry Rainsford, Tony Cottrell, Barry Bark, Nancy Gardiner, Peter Jeffery, Brian Jeffery, Michael White, Denise Kew.

Alan Rodbourne, Alfred Bond, Peter Hobbs and Brian Miles having a day out in Southsea, 1950s.

Hursley Playabouts in 1978, a group which provided village entertainments for several years. Above: standing L to R - Ron Vosper, Cicely Bull, Alan Beusmans.

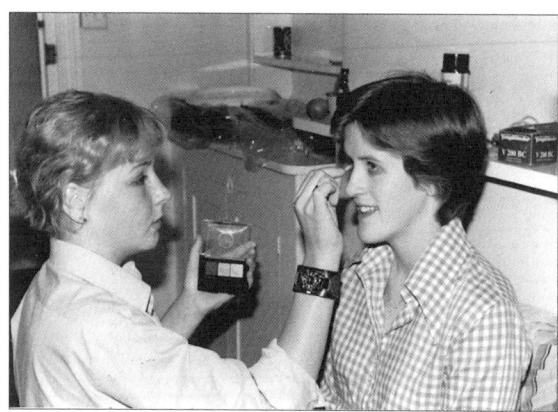

Stage make-up.
Above: Danny Rolfe and Catherine Kew;   Below: Danny Rolfe and Vincent Hawkins.

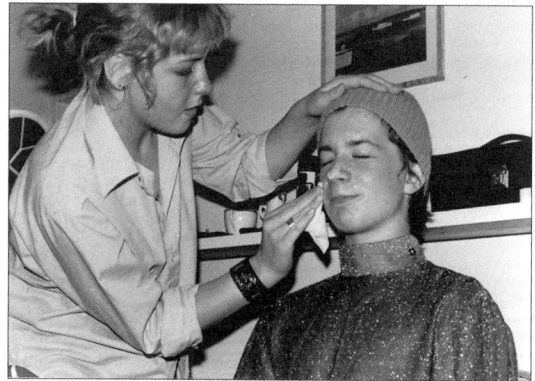

'Court Merdon Castle No. 6904 Hursley' reads the banner of the Ancient Order of Foresters Friendly Society as they gathered outside the King's Head circa 1919.

This magnificent certificate 'announces 'that Frank Alder was duly admitted a Member of the Merdon Court No. 6904 on the 1st day of February in the year 1882'.

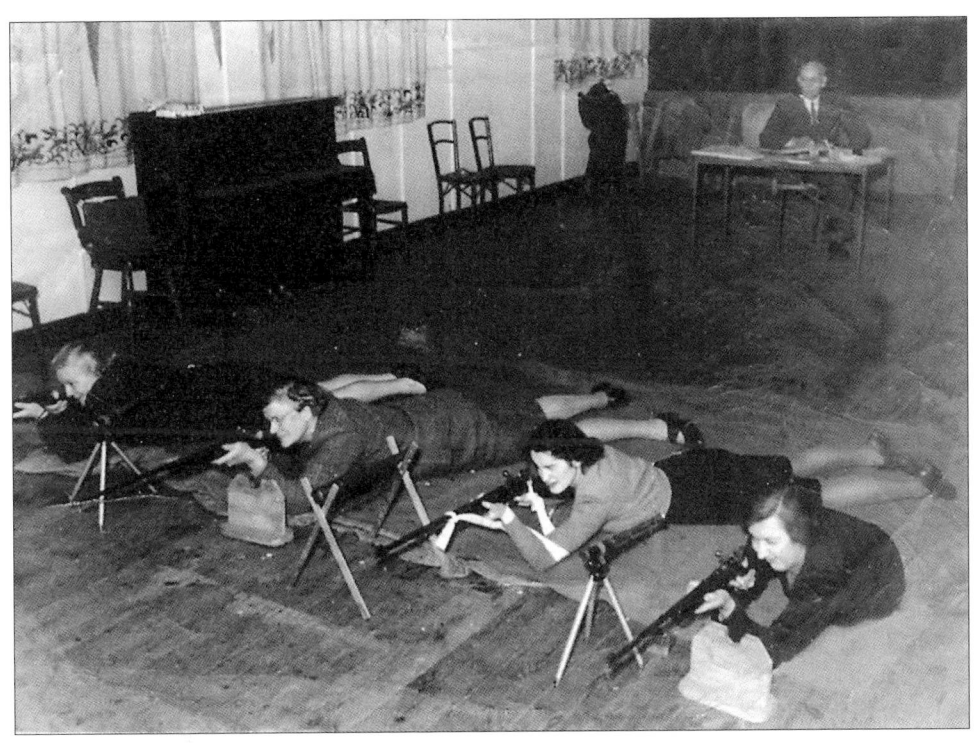

Shooting Club practice at Catways Hut in the 1930s.

Left to right: Willie and Andy Bull, Alan Beusmans and Peter Bull, 1996.

*A class in the Entertainments Hall in the 1930s.
Due to its very poor condition after the wartime occupation by Vickers, this hall had to be demolished for safety reasons.*

The children of Hursley, Christmas party 1965. **Hampshire Chronicle**

Each year the village holds a summer fete.
Above: village fete in the grounds of Southend House in the early 1960s. The group includes Michael White, Peter Whitmarsh, Barry Bark, Peter & Brian Jeffery and Nancy Gardiner.
Below: children enjoying the 1965 fete, also at Southend House.

Hampshire Chronicle

Below: Children's fancy dress competition at the 1981 village fete.

Below: on the bottle stall is Sheila Rawdon buying a ticket from Cicely Bull and Gill Edwards, 2001.

Hursley Over 60s Club, late 1950s.

Members of the Mayflower Society of America visiting All Saints' in July 2002. A number of them are descended from Stephen Hopkins who, with his wife and children, lived in Hursley before sailing on the 'Mayflower' in 1620. Included in this photo are Stan Rawdon, who presented his research on Hopkins, and other members of the congregation.

Local People at work

Hampshire County Council Farrier School visiting Hursley. It travelled the county to instruct blacksmiths in new skills. This picture was taken in the Dolphin Inn yard, in the 1920s. Vic Pavey, village blacksmith on the right, next to him is George Smith, the instructor. Bill Eades is on the extreme left.

Bill Eades at work at the forge.

This receipted invoice records the sale of Bill Eades' coal and haulage business to Martin Waldron on 1st May 1969. It reads: Received from Mr Martin Waldron the sums of £100 and £450 on account of the purchase consideration of my coal and haulage business under the terms of the agreement made between us. . . Paid with thanks £550. W G Eades.

Mrs Steiner doing her laundry outside Pelican Farm Cottage. Mid 1930s.

Alf Burrows having a break from felling elm trees at the Potters Heron.

Stan Thorne, coppersmith, in his workshop at the rear of the Pine Emporium. He retired in October 2001.

Philip H Pratt arriving at special celebrations to mark 60 years as Hursley's butcher.

Brian Cheater reopened the butcher's shop in March 2000.

Miscellaneous

An excerpt from the old Hursley Post newspaper dated 1850. These advertisements read:

WANTED:
Errand boy to make deliveries for butcher. Must be reliable, trustworthy and swift. Cycle provided. 2d a week.

Be swept off your feet!! Bob's sweep company is looking for young lads and lasses who are keen to earn a living. Preferred age between 5 and 8 years old. All enquiries made to Robert Hachitt, 23 Victoria Street, London.

Workers needed for factory floor. "Grimes and son" need hard working children to sweep the factory floors, clean machinery, etc. Long hours required, overtime necessary.

SITUATION VACANT:
Position available for young girl of 8-15 years old. Will be trained as a scullery maid, and attend to general kitchen chores. Residence is required and appropriate accommodation is provided. All enquiries should be made to Mr Mitchell, 21 Hursley Road, Hursley, Hampshire.

Alec and Beryl Kew's wedding group outside the Parish Hall. Note in the background the 16th century granary which was demolished in the 1950s.

The wedding of Augustus Sillence and Julia Stares, 1912/13. Married at All Saints' by the Revd. T Pughe, but photographed here outside Pitt Chapel where Julia was the organist. Pitt Chapel at that time was not licensed for weddings.

Ernest and Emma Wild with their children: Harry, Frank, Walter, Lizzie and Clara, taken around 1910.

Another photo of the Wild family about four years later, taken behind their home at No. 97.

Ernest in his retirement: by this time his grandson, Mike Hampton, was running a fruit and vegetable shop from the old saddlery.

Mrs Hilda Bunney, Miss Joan Percy and Mr Archie Heath, 1995.

Beryl and Maurice Bunney.

Hursley Parish Council, 2002.
Left to right: Paul Watters, Alan Beusmans, Rod Gilbert, Martin Waldron (Chairman), John Brooks (Clerk), Ros Heath, Peter Bull, John Fields.

Hursley millennium photograph exhibition, with Hazel Corney, Carol McDonnell, Antonia Hawkins and Mike McDonnell.

Presentation of a cheque for £1,305 for the All Saints' window appeal, December 2000. The money was raised from sales of the book 'Hursley 2000' by Stan Rawdon.
L to R: Stan Rawdon, Hazel Corney, Mike McDonnell.

Demonstration demanding a 30 mph speed limit through the village, March 2001. Parish Councillors being interviewed by Meridian TV, together with Bernadette Welch and Dennis Beacham.

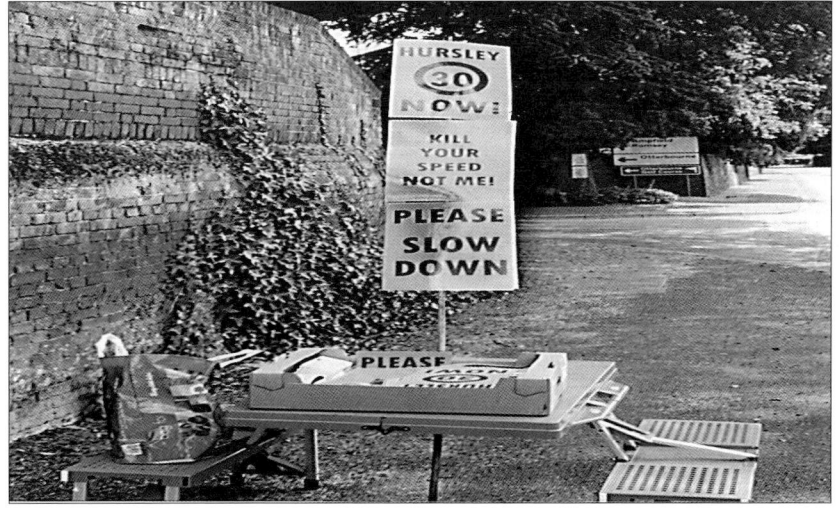

1898, this document accompanied the presentation of a dressing case to Mr Noel Baxendale, eldest son of Mr Joseph Baxendale by the above-listed tenants and employees of the Hursley Estate and the Hursley Hunt.

Local Transport

Bill Jones in his 'Scout', photo taken in Collins Lane, 26th December 1918.

Another picture of the 'Scout', the first vehicle belonging to Hursley Motor Services. It was purchased in 1912 and licensed to carry sixteen passengers or one ton of merchandise.

A tranquil view of the main road in the late nineteenth century.

The first lorry belonging to F W Jones, a Chevrolet, with driver, Bill Eades.

*Above: A. Wilson's delivery van from the bakery at South End outside the County Arms PH, Winchester, late nineteenth century.
Below: Its early twentieth century replacement.*

Martin Waldron, haulier, with his brother's 8-wheeled Seddon Atkinson Tipper, 1998.

1940s AA Box. This stood at Pound corner until it was damaged by fire and is now in the Avoncroft Museum of Buildings at Bromsgrove.

Walter Wild in 1989, taken in Bournemouth with a 1920s Italian Temrerino car which he had partially restored many years before.

The old Pitt bus shelter has found a new home as a garden summerhouse.

Three Aerial Views of the Village

Enlargement from part of an aerial photograph taken of Hursley from 4,000 feet in 1918.

Mrs Claudia Pettifer

A similar view from another aerial photograph dated 1989.

© Sky Library Wadenho Lodge, Wadenho, Peterboro'

The village centre in the 1990s.

IBM (UK) Laboratories Ltd. Hursley

Index of places

All Saints' Church: 8-10; 34; 120-128; 148; 171; 180
Ampfield: 31; 32; 156
Ampfield Wood: 29
Anmery Cottage: 46
Anmery Lodge: 28; 45
Avoncraft Museum of Buildings, Bromsgrove: 186

Berrydown Farm: 60; 106-107
Brick Kiln Cottage: 31
Bunstead Lane: 108
Butcher's shop: 175

Catways Hut: 140; 167
Church Lodge: 29; 44; 48; 57
Collins Lane: 68; 73; 183
Crabwood: 61
Cranbury Park: 105

Dog Kennel Pond: 32
Dolphin Field: 84
Dolphin Inn: 78; 83; 172
Down Farm: 113
Dummers: 114

Enmill Farm: 52
Enmill Lane: 94
Estate Brickworks: 31
Estate Dairy: 41; 51
Estate Laundry: 42
Estate Office: 42

Farley Chamberlayne Church: 116-117
Farley Chamberlayne Farm: 118
Farley Mount: 115; 140
Farley Semaphore: 119
Field House: 102-103; 130-131
Forge: 75; 79; 172-173

Girls' School: 48

Hayling Island: 142
Heathcote Mausoleum: 125
Hollyhock Cottage: 69
Home Close: 140
Home Farm: 26-27; 36-40; 52; 59
Home Farm Lodge: 42
Hursley Garage: 71; 72
Hursley Park House: 15-25; 137-138; 152; 168

Isle of Wight: 143

Jermyns House, Ampfield: 156
John Keble Primary School: 134-136; 154; 155

Keble Cottage, No 98A: 82
Keepers Lodge: 32
King Alfred's College: 142
King's Head PH: 68; 72; 73; 161; 165
Knapp Lodge: 31

Ladwell: 101-103
Longmore: 104
Lychgate: 35

Market Gardens: 85
Mayflower Society: 171
Merdon Castle: 33; 143
Merdon Cottages: 67
Merdon Lodge: 28; 45
Merdon Manor: 64-66; 132
Meredon Close: 68; 85

No. 17: 69
No. 33: 70
No. 78: 75; 77
No. 95: 78
No 95A: 77
No. 100: 86
Northend Bakery: 84
Northend shop: 70

Oaklands, Farley: 119; 132-133; 147
Old Court House: 74
Old Saddlery, No.97: 80-81; 178
Outwood Lodge: 32

Parish Hall: 29; 149; 150; 153; 176
Parsonage Farm: 108; 110-111
Pelican Court: 84; 88
Pelican Cottage: 174
Pelican Farm: 88
Pelican Inn: 88
Penfold Lodge: 29
Pine Emporium: 174

Pitt: 53; 92-97; 177
Pitt Vale Farm: 98
Police House: 87
Potter's Heron: 174
Pound Corner: 99-100; 186
Pound Cottages: 99-100

Ratlake: 31
Recreation Ground: 10-11; 151
Red House: 101

St Luke's, Stanmore: 128
Schoolmaster's House: 86
Shawlands: 109
Silkstead Farm: 112-113
Square, The: 74
Southampton Lodge: 30; 44
Southend House: 88; 169
Southend Bakery: 185
South Lynch: 91; 156
Standon: 90
Standon Farmhouse: 62; 90
Standon House: 89
Sunlight Cottages: 37; 143
Sussex Garage: 71
Swiss Cottage: 35

Vicarage: 34; 121; 123
Village Shop: 75; 76
Violet Hill Cottage: 43
Violet Hill Reservoir: 56

Winchester Lodge: 30; 47

Printed in Great Britain
by Amazon

About the Author, YvonneB

- Love Entrepreneurs (Co-founder); a unique business network aimed at creating real change in the entrepreneurial space

- Soon to be launched, Wellbeing Retreats; where women can escape to upgrade their life quality through health & fitness, personal development and relaxation in beautiful international locations

Connect with YvonneB on Facebook and Twitter @YvonneBLtd and join the YvonneB Community at

https://www.yvonnebltd.com/

With more than a 30-year history in the fitness & leisure industry, including a successful spell in figure fitness competitions, Yvonne is uniquely placed to help women combine healthy living with their personal & professional development.

Yvonne is the author of 'The Virtualholic Handbook', a guide for women seeking to enter the Virtual Assistant business world, 'Yes You Can' a personal development book for women who are open to exploring their life & business opportunities and 'Fabulously Fit & Healthy at 50', a handbook for health-conscious women in midlife.

Yvonne set up in business back in 2004/5 as a Virtual Assistant and within 2 years was also co-directing a training business. Her work took her across the UK, into Europe and as far afield as Hong Kong, delivering customised training to the leisure industry. In 2008 with the recession in flow, she made the painful decision to step down from the training business and went back to the drawing board.

Fast forward 2010 YvonneB Limited was born and Yvonne spent the next 6 years on her own personal development and health journey, learning more, working as an associate trainer and coach for a leading global company whilst developing her own courses and programmes.

2017, Yvonne now operates 3 businesses:

- YvonneB Limited; working with Gen X women who are seeking to maximise life, being their best and living their best life

About the Author, YvonneB

As an award-winning trainer, AUNLP & CMI qualified coach, Women's WorldWide Web E-mentor and owner of a national award winning training business, Yvonne Bignall is known as the Chief Confidence Officer. Her company, YvonneB Limited, is a personal & professional development company working with women to develop a health- centred lifestyle; healthy body, mind, business, relationships and beyond.

Photo & Styling: Anna Perra at Anna Perra Styling

things have the power to keep you in the victim mentally when you are the victor.

It begins with a decision. Decide to stop hiding in the shadows. Decide to start creating your life. Instead of waiting to see if life changes or if it will right the wrongs you have encountered, **YOU** make it so.

If you are not prepared to make the changes necessary in your thinking, beliefs and behaviours, then you cannot expect positive change to come.

Your life is in your hands. Suck it up or change.

Unlock your potential and live the life you deserve and desire;

if you truly want a better life, YOU create it...

- You carefully chose who you surrounded yourself with; loving family, friends and like-minded people? How much more love would you have in your life and how might those strong connections impact your wellbeing and achievements; what value might that add to your life?

- You did something that made someone else feel thankful for having you in their life; acknowledging the difference you make, helping you realise your true value?

- You got up each day and had fun! Imagine the joy of focusing on activities that brought more laughter into your world, people smiling back at you, so attracted to your energy?

- You had faith in something or someone and that faith supported you through your darkest, hardest days? Imagine the power of that overwhelming love, a sense that everything will be okay through faith, allowing you to let go of doubt, watching it float away like a balloon set free?

Just imagine that… how much better would your life be? How much closer to being your best you would you be?

Each of the 7F principles plays an essential role in helping you create the life you desire. They are connected and as you improve in one area other areas are impacted.

It is time to take responsibility for where your life is right now. No more blaming, no more hiding and no self-pitying. These

Wherever you are now, one small change could be all you need to take to propel into a better place. Look at yourself in the mirror; who are you right now, and who are you at your best?

Imagine making a small change, a shift that moved you forward so that you could view the world differently than you do in your current state. What if:

- You changed your daily routine by taking the time to begin your health care journey. If you were 10%, 20%, even 30% fitter and healthier than you are right now, how might that impact your physiological state, your self-confidence, self-esteem, that underpinning certainty that you are doing something positive for your survival, secure in the knowledge that the wonderful free gifts of mind and body are being trained to work optimally for your best life?

- You willingly took on challenges that stretched you, expanding your comfort zone; how might that free your mind from the limiting beliefs, judgements and expectations you carry. How might that impact the experience of self and life required to grow and develop?

- You could develop a clear picture of what freedom means to you, based on YOUR goals, YOUR dreams and you took daily steps to achieve them; better finances, starting your own business, being able to work anywhere in the world, meeting your dream partner? Imagine the wonderful discoveries you would make along the journey.

CHAPTER 11
The Time for Change Is Now

Whichever area of your life you fail to focus on, to pay real attention to and action, can send you spiralling down to places you do not want to be in. The spiral moves you away from being your best you and from creating your best life.

You will have noticed health is the common denominator through all these principles and every downward spiral ends up impacting your mental and physical wellbeing. This highlights the importance of putting your health first, always. It is not about looking good it is about building the mental, physical, emotional and spiritual strength required to create the life you desire; to help you manoeuvre through your life utilising the amazing gifts you are blessed with; mind, body, and soul.

When your life goes out of sync and you fail to do what needs to be done to address it, the stress on your health accumulates.

But imagine what would happen if you could flip those spirals and instead of constantly sliding down, you were constantly climbing up to being your best self in all areas of your life?

By focusing in on your mental, physical, spiritual and emotional wellbeing it is possible; they have the power to propel you into the life you desire whilst also teaching you key lessons on how to better manage the challenges you are likely to face on your journey through life; doubt, stress, limiting beliefs. Think what you might be able to create in your life with such a powerful toolkit.

Having Faith

No one can make you have faith. You can, however, choose faith. When life sucks, faith steps in. I warmed to this verse from the bible as I thought about the importance of faith:

'Faith. It doesn't make things easy, it makes them possible'

Luke: 1:37

Decide faith matters to you and know that difficulties in life are lessons not some form of punishment. Move past the 'why me' cry. Believe that faith guides you; the lower you go the deeper you dig in to get back up and faith provides the strength to do so.

Faith brings breakthroughs. It reduces limiting beliefs because it allows you to accept that uncertainty is okay, that you don't have to follow the crowd and it gives you the freedom to let go and just be.

Faith isn't a religion, it's a decision…

Clinical Depression and More

Without action and treatment, this self-pity can lead to clinical depression. Seeing anything good in your life is like hunting for a needle in a haystack and you haven't got the energy for that.

The clinical depression, if left untreated, could increase the potential misuse of alcohol and drugs, lead to insomnia as well as weight loss or weight gain.

This is not an experience you want to have or a state you want to stay in. You must seek out the help you need to claim back your life and begin to believe life has more for you.

Remember:

- Depression is a common mental disorder. Globally, an estimated 350 million people of all ages suffer from depression

- Depression is the leading cause of disability worldwide and is a major contributor to the overall global burden of disease

- More women are affected by depression than men

- At its worst, depression can lead to suicide

The good news; there are effective treatments for depression

on and believe. Before you know it, what you believe becomes your reality.

Creating What You Don't Want

As you see each negative 'what if' form to become something real in your life, you confirm to yourself and others that there is no point in having faith, no point in having hope because you have proof to the contrary. Everything you didn't want has appeared, proof enough that life just sucks.

What you fail to see is your constant focus on what you don't want, the energy and belief you tie into that focus. You have energized your thoughts into creation, and these are the very things you didn't want.

From here it is easy to fall into self-pity, resentment, and distrust of anything that indicates life could be better. There is little hope. As far as you are concerned, hope doesn't exist in your world.

What you don't see is by giving in to self-pity and turning your back on life's possibilities, you are refusing to take responsibility for your life or control of it.

In this self-absorbed state, you are drawn to being the victim, of showing others how hard life is, how there is no hope. You have stopped believing in yourself and begun to develop an inferiority complex. You whine continuously, you fill your life with negativity and anyone else's who will listen, and prolonged, it begins to impact your wellbeing.

Living A Limited Life

Instead of exploring and living life to the full you limit everything. In doing so you limit your beliefs as well as your actions. And because limits are your norm, you often tell others to do the same, discouraging them from exploring their potential. You think you are doing them a favour but you're not.

There is discomfort in this limited living. At times, you watch others make big strides forward and either wish for the same or wish you had their strength, knowledge, drive; faith. But you don't. When you imagine achieving anything you automatically revert to what will go wrong, what won't happen. Your focus is on the negative.

Focusing on What You Don't Want

Where others see possibilities to grow, develop and succeed, you see the possibility to appear stupid or fail. The visions in your mind show you how impossible things are. When you think 'what if' it always ends with all the things that could go wrong; what if I fail? What if no one likes me? What if I can't do the job? What if, what if, what if…

What if it all went your way? That's not a thought that lingers with you if it arrives at all.

And as you focus in and join the dots of all these negative what if's, you begin to believe them. They are no longer just thoughts they are a set of beliefs. The thing is, the mind, being as powerful as it is, will begin to search out to find that which you think, focus

- Feel out of control as more of what you don't want in your life appears in it

- Impact your health

Right Now

Right now, you might be avoiding doing anything that challenges what you know with certainty is within your capability. You tread through life very carefully, not wanting to disturb anything or anyone. You shy away from new opportunities, in fact, you do it so much you barely ever see them anymore.

You are living a shadow of the life that is possible for you because it feels like the only safe thing you can do. Any type of change throws you into a panic without anything to hold on to. Fear has become your natural default. You don't like it but you feel unable to change it.

Living in Constant Uncertainty

Welcome to the world where anything could change in a heartbeat. Whilst you know each moment could change the landscape of the day or even your life, internally you fight the knowledge and search instead for the certain and predictable.

You fear change, the unknown and struggle to understand how others embrace these things. You do all that you can to maintain routine and avoid doing anything that might bring about a different outcome or experience. In this place, sameness feels safe and requires no faith.

through your life lessons, the pain-filled days, you would not be standing today. Somehow, you made it through, in faith.

How You Fail to Have Faith

Having faith often requires you to invest your hopes and belief in something unseen, not tangible. That may not hold any logical sense to you and therefore doing it, having that kind of faith, becomes a challenge.

In seeing faith as a challenge, you move away from it by:

- Living life with limitations

- Living life fearfully

- Feeling out of control

- Being stressed and anxious

The Downward Spiral

To wake up every day with no faith leaves you with little if any hope. And with no hope, what is the point? As you approach each day you are likely to be expecting the worst because the worst appears to keep on coming and soon enough you begin to:

- Constantly feel uncertain

- Limit your life experiences to limit the potential outcomes

- Become overly anxious, operating from a 'what if' fear-filled perspective

confidence in someone or something; be it based on religious beliefs, an inner spiritual sense or by choice.

"Belief is rooted in the mind; faith is rooted in the heart and faith is the hope beyond your conscious thinking"

It is through faith that you:

- Find the strength to get through the hardest of days

- Do what is necessary to take better care of yourself

- Pull yourself up when you have been knocked down

- Emerge from being someone into being your best self

- Give knowing you will receive and reap what you sow

- Do things you do not know, with certainty, you can do

When you are going through your most challenging moments who do you turn to? Where do you seek wisdom, understanding, help? These indicate your sources of faith.

With a never-ending stream of life lessons, issues, challenges, and painful circumstances, developing faith provides you with the ability to let go of worry and instead hope and believe that everything is as it should be in this moment and that change for the better is possible.

For all that you have been through to date you have survived, you are still standing. You are stronger than you think and you can help others because of it. Had you not had a source of faith to get

CHAPTER 10
Having Faith

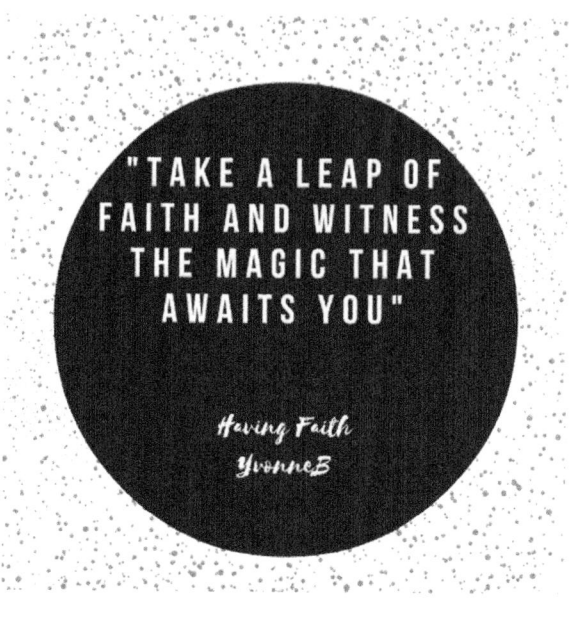

Faith is a personal matter and we have the choice to decide who and what we have faith in. The important thing is to develop faith, as it allows you to step into opportunities you might not otherwise take.

As someone who believes in God, faith comes easily as I look to a higher power. However, I also believe in having faith in who I am, in human kindness, in the universal laws of our world, believing that all situations can be resolved, all changes can be made and all people can be helped.

Faith keeps hope alive and as human beings hope is essential to wellbeing. Without hope, we are lost. Faith is complete trust and

lower blood pressure, lower levels of the stress hormone cortisol and slimmer waistlines. There is no coincidence in these findings; fun is a crucial part of your wellbeing. Add laughter to that fun and the benefits multiply. Take all the fun and laughter away and it is not surprising life appears to suck.

Having Fun

Fun and laughter are free medicinal cures. You don't have to get a prescription, you just decide to bring more of them into your life.

What difference would some fun bring to your life right now? Imagine how good you would feel having fun and laughing every day. No one expects you to spend all your time rolling about on the floor holding your belly, but having the ability to dip in and out of this high-frequency state can completely change the way you look at life and experience life.

Having fun is good for you physically, mentally, emotionally and socially. It can strengthen relationships, disperse disagreements, relax you, release your inhibitions and frees you to be you, improve moods as well as boost your immune system.

Even in the world of academia laughter is recognised as central to human condition with its ability to act as a coping mechanism. Whatever purpose you believe it serves, know it serves you well.

The Ever, Present Grey Cloud

The lack of connection with others sees your moods shifting into a dark place. It feels difficult to get out of moods, they feel unbreakable. You get stuck in a state.

When you lose the ability to break a state, that is, get out of a frame of mind to enter a more appropriate one, you end up living in rewind land where you keep playing the same situation, issue or problem repeatedly. You never get to a solution because your present state doesn't lead you to one.

From here on in the grey cloud gets bigger and darker. You become miserable, moving you further away from fun, laughter, and joyfulness. And before you know it, your health is impacted.

The Funny Thing About Health

If fun and laughing have the power to heal and help you cope with life's more stressful situations, what do you think happens when you don't have them in your life? You get stressed more easily and stress can lead you to:

- Poor sleeping

- Poor diet

- Increased disease risk

Psychosomatic Medicine published a study back in 2009 where people were assessed on how frequently they engaged in 10 different types of activities. Of those assessed, the people who had the most fun were found to have a smaller body mass index (BMI),

Feeling Excluded

There is laughter around you, a lightness in the mood but you don't feel it. The more you see others having fun, the more detached you feel. And suddenly you are not part of the scene anymore. You feel excluded but you have excluded yourself.

When you feel socially excluded;

- It prevents you from improving your social skills and that impacts your ability to read and interact with others

- It impacts your emotional wellbeing. You have fewer positive behaviours to mirror and begin to slip into more negative beliefs and behaviours

- It becomes more difficult to break down barriers with others. In fact, you are more likely to shut them out and see yourself as different, damaging relationships instead of building them

No Friends Please, I'm Serious

Before you know it, you can count your friends on one finger. Your desire to be taken seriously, disengages others and they steer clear of you.

It might not bother you at first, after all, they are the jokers in the pack and you are not. But think about it; suddenly your network shrinks and you have more and more time on your own.

You don't laugh, you certainly don't crack jokes and you find people that do tedious.

Right Now

For many reasons, fun might be on the back burner right now. You may have more pressing life concerns; relationships, career choices, your health. However, fun can help you decipher what to do next in many of the problematic situations you find yourself in just by getting you into a more relaxed state where you can view life in a more balanced way.

You might already be feeling stressed and fun might be the last thing on your mind. Maybe you haven't had a good laugh for a long time and as you look at life see little to laugh about.

Whatever point you are at right now, continuing to disregard fun is unlikely to help you shift out of your current state.

Your Declining Creativity and Productivity

Creativity comes from the freedom to imagine the possibilities without barriers. As you resign yourself to not having fun or seeing it as important, you impact your ability to be imaginative, to let go and just be. This not only has the potential to affect your work life, it might stifle your ability to do fun things with your kids, with your partner and with your family and friends.

Fun is also good for your wellbeing so by shutting it down, you negatively impact your wellbeing and that, in turn, impacts your productivity. But instead of realising this and relaxing into having fun to revive your wellbeing, you pressure yourself into doing more work, believing that being more serious is the solution. This can often lead to feeling burnt out and excluded. Because all around you people are finding time to have fun.

You fail to have fun when you:

- Take everything in life seriously

- Do not see the value in being able to laugh at yourself sometimes

- See others as immature when they are having fun

- Become offended by others who are having fun

The Downward Spiral

If you are not making fun a priority in your life, then watch out. Just like the other principles, it too has a downward spiral.

A lack of fun is linked to:

- A decline in creativity and productivity

- Feelings of exclusion

- Being less sociable

- Finding it difficult to shift bad moods

- Increased health issues; obesity, blood pressure, stress hormones, cardiac health, low sense of wellbeing

There is no one or right way to have fun but a life without it is not a life at all.

- Reduce the intensity of worries and stress

- Stimulate your creativity

- Increase your productivity

- Give you a clearer perspective

It's Time for Unstructured Play

In a life where you do so much by rules and deadlines, constantly conforming, having fun releases you from those behaviours and allows you to be childlike again; free, creative and dreamlike.

Having fun plays an important role in bonding with others, creating memories, lifting your mood and living in the now. It is important to define what fun means to you and make it happen in your life.

By choosing to not have fun you are negating the many benefits it brings to your relationships, health and wellbeing, and life in general.

How You Fail to Have Fun

It is not difficult to have fun, to laugh out loud, to crack a joke. Yet as you get older it is too easy to see fun as something kids have. When you reach adulthood playfulness suddenly gets pushed to the back of the 'things to do' list and suddenly life becomes more serious.

say they haven't got time to do more of what they love; unless it's to watch more TV, of course.

It's time for a change. TV can be overwhelmingly depressing, pouring out negative messages at a rate you can barely keep up with or serving up brain deadening programmes that barely stimulate a brain cell. Yes, there are some great programmes too and a good comedy goes a long way in the pursuit of laughter. However, do you honestly want to while away the precious hours of your life stuck in front of a box? Or do you want to spend time living your life to the full?

Fun is powerful

It can:

- Make you feel more centred, alive, connected, energised, peaceful and relaxed

- Create experiences, not just outcomes

- Encourage active pursuits positively impacting your health

- Be shared with others

- Change your mood or state in record time; it has a positive physiological impact

- Create positive feelings through the increase of endorphins; neurotransmitters

- Be healing when there have been disagreements and fallouts

CHAPTER 9
Having Fun

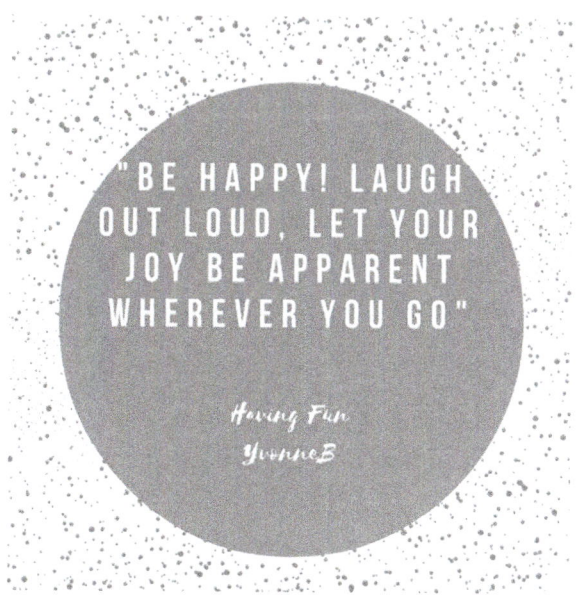

"BE HAPPY! LAUGH OUT LOUD, LET YOUR JOY BE APPARENT WHEREVER YOU GO"

Having Fun
YvonneB

Fun! One of my favourite words of all time, and one that too many people don't take seriously.

Having Fun is tied to doing more of what you love. It provides an opportunity to enjoy life and experience the joy you were encouraged to have in childhood.

When we are having fun, we are often learning more because we are relaxed. Therefore, fun is not purely an after-work activity or play time with the kid's; play positively affects you, others and the environment.

Research has shown that the average household watches more than 5 hours of TV per day. Interesting then, when you hear people

Paying It Forward

Something as simple as contributing can positively impact your life. It can help you discover your purpose, it can connect you to people who have similar values and it helps others.

It might not always be clear to you what you can do, but starting somewhere is the key. Every day there are people and causes in need of help and support. They are not seeking perfection or huge changes; they simply need care, love, and attention. And if ever you wanted to shake off that feeling of not being enough, paying it forward provides it.

When you pay it forward you make a difference:

- You help someone else without expecting anything in return

- The recipient feels good because someone cares

- You feel good because you have made a difference

- Gratitude is experienced more frequently by you and others

- A ripple effect of generosity flows and its reach is likely to be much wider than you can imagine

- It increases your well-being by decreasing stress, helping to lower blood pressure, potentially extending your life span

- It increases your happiness and gives you a sense of purpose and life satisfaction

Don't put off another day wondering what you can do to contribute. Start right where you are, right now.

Moments of Loneliness and Unfulfillment

You ignore your gut messages but now you begin to feel something is missing from your life. There is something you need to be doing yet you are unable to identify it.

It's weird because you have begun to experience feelings of loneliness and unfulfillment even when you are in good company and doing things. There is an emptiness that you just can't describe or find a valid reason for. It could be a desire that is not being nurtured or hopes that have been left behind.

This is a key moment to reflect on your feelings and what you are doing to fulfill your higher purpose. If you are feeling lonely it could be that you are not spending enough time with people who share the same values as you. If you are not fulfilled it might be that you are unaligned with what truly matters to you or you are not reaching out to someone in the spirit of generosity.

Your desire to contribute is often tied to being with people who have similar beliefs in matters that mean the most to you; the wellbeing of the planet, eradicating poverty, safety of children.

And like so many other areas of life, if your ability to contribute remains unfulfilled your health could suffer.

The Unhealthy Health Card

Your inner voice full of negative messages about your abilities and lack of contribution turn into feelings of stress and, when compounded by other life stresses, can go on to impact the wellbeing of your immune system leading to other health issues.

that you replay every time you don't do something you said you would or wanted to. Before you know it, you have an internal playlist of all the things you can't do, people you should have helped but didn't and your unhappiness deepens.

At this point, you can turn the tables and look for a way to contribute. Or you can stay feeling stuck by ignoring your feelings.

Ignoring Your Gut Instinct

You haven't given up on the idea of doing something only now you are looking to do it from a place of guilt, dissatisfaction, and unhappiness. With all these negative feelings to manage the voice telling you what you can do is easily drowned out by the constant, 'you can't' messages based on your lack of action to date.

Your gut instinct kicks in; that deep sense of knowing you have something to do, to give but because there is no logical connection, it doesn't make sense at a conscious level, you try to ignore it.

When your gut starts creating feelings to do something, it wants you to listen. Your gut instinct has the capacity to read a minuscule message you wouldn't otherwise be aware of. And when you ignore it, you dismiss the power of your internal system.

You can 'trust your gut instinct' or you can expect more negative feelings to follow.

- Without realising it, you negatively impact your health by not helping others; leaving you more susceptible to stress, disease, and depression

Underselling Your Abilities

It is all too easy to undervalue what you can do, especially when you believe it takes huge actions to bring about any meaningful change. In fact, it is often the sum of all the little changes that create the meaningful change.

You tell yourself you don't have money to help others as if money is the only resource others need that you have. You take your skills for granted and instead of seeing how they might help a person, you assume there is someone who can do what you do better, quicker, more professionally and that leads you to not bothering to do anything. It pains you because you want to make a difference but you allow life to get in the way and you move on...

Dissatisfied and Unhappy

It begins to play on your mind, sometimes prompted by something you see, maybe an advert for a charity on TV, or an article in the local paper about an elderly person in your neighbourhood who couldn't get any assistance to do their day to day tasks. You then proceed to feed yourself unhelpful negative messages out of guilt and that leads to dissatisfaction with your decision not to do anything, making you unhappy.

Whilst these feelings might not hang around for long, every time you feel them you build up a reserve of negative messages

a difference. You consider signing up to a monthly subscription cause but spend so much time worrying about whether the money gets to the people who need it most, you end up not doing anything.

It might be more profound than that. You feel as if you have a need to be contributing in a real and meaningful way but have no clue what that looks like. And because you have no clarity you try to ignore the feeling or end up doing all manner of things in the hope that one of them will feel right.

You might even be in that place where you don't see the point because it's not your problem; you have got enough going on in your life so stopping to worry about someone else is not on the cards.

Wherever you are right now, your willingness or lack thereof to do for others could send you down another spiral that impacts your long-term wellbeing.

- You undersell your ability to make a difference

- You feel guilty, unhappy and dissatisfied at your lack of decision making to contribute in some way

- Your gut instinct tells you your contribution matters but struggling to identify what the contribution is, freezes you into a state of inaction

- You experience moments of loneliness as you fail to explore ways to provide values-driven service

- Believe community issues are for Governments to fix

- Believe things like poverty can't be solved

The Downward Spiral

Paying it forward provides an outlet for your spiritual wellbeing, your kindness, and generosity; often places where you experience a true sense of serving others. Not only is serving others good for your health, it helps you manage stress, it increases your happiness and it helps you to experience gratitude.

Without finding an outlet to experience these high energy vibrational states you are likely to:

- Miss out on the chance to influence others to give back, reducing the ripple effect

- Miss out on the happiness factors associated with helping others

- Struggle to find your sense of purpose and satisfaction

- More easily be affected by loneliness as giving back enhances your social life

- Fall into health issues associated with loneliness, including stress

Right Now

You might be considering doing something to help others but you feel that you don't have the time or can't do enough to make

By actively seeking to pay if forward you can recognise:

- The many opportunities there are to help someone else

- If you are being too self-absorbed and break the focus

- Ways to end complacency as you seek out ways to contribute instead

- Your own abilities, strengths, values and desires to make a difference in the world

By paying it forward you are ultimately ensuring that your contribution has the widest possible results. By doing a good deed for someone, no matter the size, and encouraging them to pass it on to another, it is possible to change communities, countries, the world.

How you Fail

Depending on your current situation and whether you see giving back only in financial terms, there are multiple ways you might be failing in paying it forward – You:

- Have got enough problems of your own to deal with

- Don't think you have the time

- Don't have any ideas on how you can contribute or make a difference

- Think your donation, be it time or money, is too small to make any significant difference

ensuring you live your life beyond yourself expecting nothing in return; and note I say beyond yourself, not instead of yourself. The truth in paying it forward is you reap what you sow; so, sow well.

You are connected to others whether you know it or not, like it or not and every action you take, every decision you make, has an impact outside of you. When you give of your time, knowledge, wealth you create a ripple effect of kindness that goes further than the eye can see, reaching more people in need than you can imagine.

In paying forward you fulfill your human need to contribute, connect, serve and experience your significance.

Giving from a place of gratitude

Sometimes a bit of time dedicated toward others, especially those not quite as connected, in good health or as well off in their lives as you, helps you realize how fortunate you are. Doing something good for someone else makes you feel good inside whilst showing them someone cares. And in that moment gratitude is experienced.

How fortunate are you to be able to help someone? How fortunate are you to be able to make a difference? These are reasons to be thankful for what you have and where you are right now, even if you feel far removed from where you want to be.

CHAPTER 8
Paying It Forward

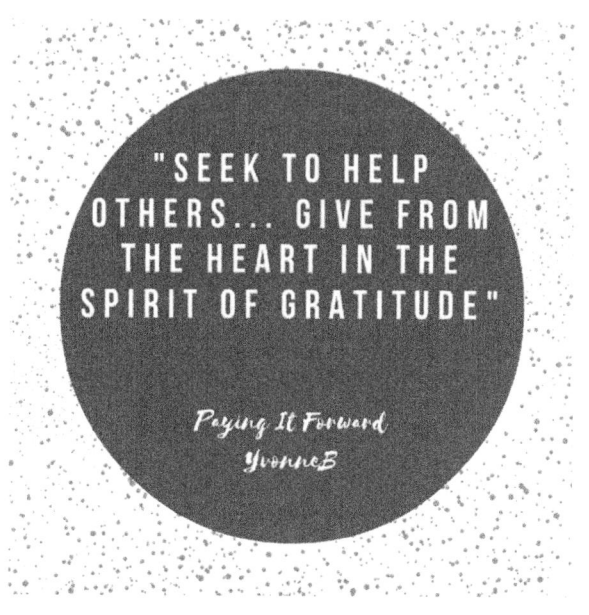

Pay it Forward was the title of a book released in 1999 adapted for film in 2000; and if you haven't seen it, it's a must. It tells the story of a young boy dealing with life with his alcoholic mother, meeting a new school teacher who sets a challenging school term project for his class and ultimately, the legacy he leaves behind by completing the project. Blending the highs and lows together seamlessly the film takes you on a heart-warming journey filled with moments of sadness and life reflection. But the story also shows how one random act of human kindness can positively affect many lives.

Paying it forward encompasses the many acts of kindness you can do to give back to your community. It is the essential part of

Family, Friends & Your Network

- Give you nothing while taking everything

- Bring more drama into your life than a TV soap

- Be full of dishonesty if being so is beneficial to the toxic person

- Be full of blame, pointing to others and circumstances

Build your relationships wisely with your eyes wide open… and begin with your relationship with you; self-love is essential to being your best you.

In the workplace, you require your colleagues to get the job done; it's called teamwork. In business, you require staff to make your business vision a success. Therefore, in daily life you need people to love, support, encourage, challenge and invigorate you, not drain you. Not everyone will deliver in all areas hence there is a need to develop a wide and varied network. But no matter how large or small that network is, the important thing is to maintain a sense of self; who you are.

Do not get lost in other people's worlds. Remain connected to your values, your dreams, your goals and what matters to you. In fact, the abler you are to do this, the less likely you are to end up in the downward spiral.

A life without healthy social connections can:

- Be detrimental to your health; more so than obesity, smoking, and high blood pressure studies have revealed

- Weaken your immune system

- Increase your rate of anxiety and depression and reduce self-esteem

And if you allow toxic relationships to stay in your life, expect them to:

- Sap your energy at every given opportunity

- Leave you open to being controlled

- Disrespect your boundaries

hormone, does the same at the other end of the scale. And you sink into despair.

The Lonely Road to Despair

Your new companion is despair, the complete loss of hope. You see no bright future, no joy and hold no expectations of being able to move forward. You feel as if your life has lost all meaning and wonder if there is any point in trying to change.

The Impact on Your Health

In a state of despair, you are likely to struggle with eating, have little solid sleep and feel more detached from people than ever, creating a void in your life. Change is the essential lifeline to winning back you, reconnecting with the people who truly love and care about you and ditching the toxic people who have contributed to your downward spiral.

Family, Friends & Your Network

Most if not all relationships begin in good faith, where trust is part of the building block. However, it is essential to be aware of the direction relationships are heading in. Are they serving you well? Are you serving them well? Are you free to be you in them? Are you able to maintain control over the things that matter to you?

As human beings, the feeling of belonging is a vital one that requires frequent positive interaction on an ongoing basis.

The Doormat Syndrome

Now it's official, you have become the go-to person for all things to complain, moan, scream and shout about. People see you listening to all the bad news and assume it is because you want to or, for the toxic brigade, because they want you to. You become a doormat for others, soaking up the pessimistic views of others, allowing them to wipe their mess all over you like the front door mat.

Lifeless in your approach, you escape further into yourself, seeking to shut out the noise. And you notice the emptiness inside of you.

Who Are You?

Heavy with what feels like the weight of the world, you seek to connect with you. Somewhere beneath all the layers of others thoughts, dramas, worries, beliefs, you exist, but you are a long way down and your numbness prevents you from digging too deep. For the first time in a long time, you miss you. You long for the person who had some degree of balance in life and could think and feel for themselves. You want it back but feel you lack the strength to do anything about it.

Your hormones might be adding to the mix of feelings too with cortisol and oxytocin imbalances. Chronic high levels of cortisol, the life-saving hormone, makes it easier to detach from others whilst low levels of oxytocin, the love, bonding & connection

blame others, content when putting others down, lie to fit their needs, hang on to anyone who is crazy enough to listen to them and at the very worst end of the scale, rule relationships through fear.

If ever there was a time to reclaim your sense of self, right here, right now would be good. You can either release that pent-up anger and frustration and get back on track or keep on sliding down.

Low Self Worth

You kept silent and now your self-worth is at an all-time low. You loathe your thoughts and your actions. You can no longer see the value you bring because, as far as you are concerned, you don't bring any. Even when the people who love you the most tell you how amazing you are, you don't hear it. You are so full of anger at who you have become and so unforgiving of the wrong turns you have made, you fall into acceptance of being unworthy of anything more.

The internal critic plays at full volume and you fall into its trap, listening and believing every word it throws at you. Your moods are uncontrollable, swinging along the scale between total calm and rage, usually focused on yourself. You reprimand yourself for being weak, not having what it takes to change the situation and then settle back into the role of the victim. It's a sad and lonely place to be.

your expressions all along. How do you get back that which was in your control? And what if by taking it back, you lose the people in your life? After all, they like you for the person you have become, not you.

You need to be liked, it is the one certainty for you right now and if that means having to bend over backward for others, so be it. But this only leads to you living a shell of a life, operated by fear and external forces with a total disregard for your true self. And it gets worse.

Living in A Toxic World

Now that you have handed over your power, you can expect toxic people to flow into your world and take up residence. It is a lot easier for them to break someone down who is already breaking than chipping away at someone who values themselves.

Once inside your world, and remember toxic people are everywhere and can be found in all types of relationships, they will serve to break your dreams, crush your hopes and remind you that you are no better than anyone else. You are not special. They suck you dry with their dramas whilst expecting you to give them 100% attention until they are done. The reality is, you are so tired, you meet their needs without any resistance. You are left feeling drained yet pleased to have helped; so, what if your needs weren't met?

Toxic people are selfish, surrounded with drama, never responsible for any of the stuff that goes on in their life, quick to turn, feels as if you are deceiving yourself or being dishonest with yourself and to manage those feelings you do more for others to make yourself feel better.

You become so lost in your relationship with others as a wife, mother, sister, colleague, friend, you forget to keep in touch with who you are and what you want or need. Before you know it, you are this other person, the one who agrees with others opinions because it's easier than sharing your own, says yes to everything to save arguments, and stops expressing true emotions because when you do it appears to bother others. In and of themselves these might not appear like game changers but every time you hold back your thoughts, opinions, and emotions, the essence of you is chipped away.

As you learn to let go of what matters to you, you feel the loss. You know you can claim back your voice and be heard but you are anxious now, unsure if now is a good time to start expressing yourself having managed not to say anything of your own thinking for some time. You decide it's easier to leave things as they are.

What brews below the surface is frustration, resentment and potentially, anger; all of which will leak out at some point, in some way.

Let Go of Your Power

Having spent enough time not being you the thought of suddenly standing up for yourself brings feelings of discomfort. You now feel guilty and ashamed for not having been honest in

- Become a doormat, soaking up people's negativity, people pleasing in your desperation to hold on to relationships even if they are not good for you

- Lose yourself and become a shell of your former self with low confidence, and little self-belief

- Allow despair to creep in and you end up trusting no one. You become lonely and detached

- Notice your health is deteriorating and your energy is flat

Right Now

There are things in your life you are not happy with. Perhaps your intimate relationship isn't going well or a friendship appears to be strained. It might even be family relationships that are struggling. The only certainty right now is that you feel the need to tiptoe around people to keep the peace, trying to meet everyone's demands. Simply put, you are unhappy but do not want to express that unhappiness. So instead you continue as if all is well, doing for others, forgetting to meet your own needs and losing your sense of self. You tell yourself if everyone else is okay it's fine but it is the beginning of another slippery slope.

Lack of Authenticity

Authenticity is your ability to own your actions, thoughts, needs, and desires. And whilst there is a great joy to be had in serving others when you forget or stop paying attention to your own needs and wants it can easily lead to inauthenticity. This, in

- You spend all your time people pleasing; not being you

- You create expectations based on your behaviours, not theirs and they are not you

The Downward Spiral of Unnurtured Relationships

Relationships can be challenging; more reason to be vigilant with who you have around you. Failing to do so can lead to circumstances in which you become a victim. Things begin to unravel when you:

- Feel you should be more than you are or need to act perfectly to meet the expectations and needs of others. You think your authentic self is not enough and you end up playing the role of someone else. This leads to loving yourself less and losing your sense of self

- Allow others to control you; you hand them your power, out of guilt, shame or a desire to be liked and then end up using statements like 'you make me feel, do, say' when their words or behaviours upset you

- Allow toxic people to settle into your life, allowing them to project their negative emotions and dramas onto you, leaving you feeling resentful and uncomfortable

- Begin to devalue yourself, questioning your own capabilities, changing your thoughts to fit others and accepting what others tell you; you follow the herd

- People who you trust and admire - Potential mentors, teachers, and coaches *Emma Hills,*

At the end of the day, connecting with others allows you to love and love is a human need.

How You Fail Yourself & Your Network

Never has it been so easy to keep in touch with people. Social media has given a helping hand both personally and professionally. There are few excuses that cut it these days for not staying in touch, even if it's a monthly Skype call, a quick 'hi, hope all is okay' text; something. Relationships won't develop where attention is lacking.

Relationships fail for a myriad of reasons. Some of the most common ways to fail your relationships are you:

- Fail to love you and realise your value; so, you end up settling for any type of relationship that comes your way

- Over commit on your promises; putting everyone's needs before your own

- You compare the people in your life as if they should all fit one size

- You expect everyone who comes into your life, to stay in your life and get out of sorts when relationships end

- You spend more time trying to fix people than accept them for who they are

- You allow toxic people to get in and hang out in your space

- Choose carefully who you place in your network

- Decide how much time you spend with the people in your network

- Ensure you give time to nurturing each of your high-value relationships

Without a support network, your own ability to grow is stifled. As you begin to look at your network check to see if these key attributes of a healthy network are present:

- People you love – your closest family and friends *Kim, Sheila, Marie, Ham, Paula, TBD*

- People you work with or for – your colleagues, associates, business partners *Dianne, Alfie, Mr Ant*

- People you have fun with - mood changing relationships *Nicky, Em, Becky, Sue, Chris, Frank*

- People from different backgrounds and cultures - seeing the world through different eyes *Sam, Marcello, Bryn?*

- People of different ages – expanding the history of life *- Pie*

- People who live in different parts of the world – enriching your understanding of the world around you *Marcela*

- People who see life differently from you - challenging each other's perceptions *Mr. Ant, FFF*

- People with different skill sets and abilities - leveraging each other's potential *Hachy*

constantly giving and the other constantly taking, causing an imbalance and resentment.

Of course, the challenging part of relationships is that you are dealing with people. And people come with their varying emotions, life baggage, mindsets, and attitudes. Furthermore, some people will show you just enough of themselves to win you over before revealing other sides of themselves that are not so enchanting.

This doesn't mean that every relationship is a search for perfection. Being able to accept people for who they are is important, as is being able to spot those with ulterior motives, manipulating habits, and narcissistic behaviours. This is where emotional intelligence comes into its own, the ability to be self-aware and aware of others.

Here's the thing; you can learn lessons from every type of relationship; good, bad or indifferent. You are just as likely to learn about human behaviour when someone does something to offend you as you are when someone is loving and kind towards you. Learning to value these experiences as lessons are key because they can either help you to grow, be stronger, more independent, more understanding and kinder or hinder you and close you down as you begin to trust others less.

It has been said that 'your network is your net worth', meaning you are the sum of the people you spend the most time with. Therefore, it pays to:

CHAPTER 7
Family, Friends & Your Network

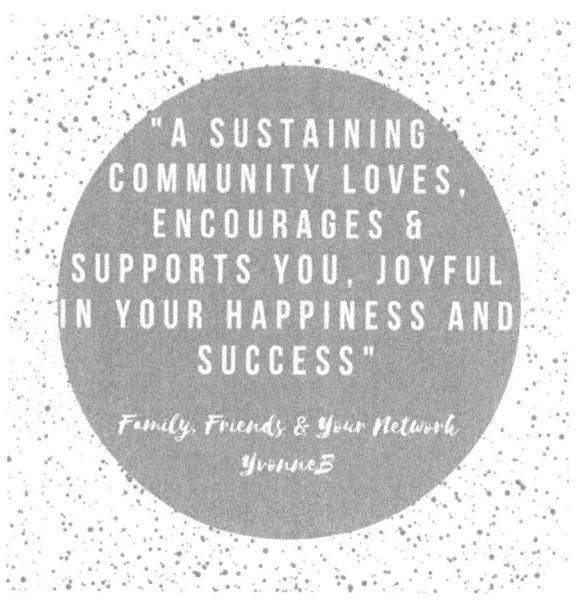

"A SUSTAINING COMMUNITY LOVES, ENCOURAGES & SUPPORTS YOU, JOYFUL IN YOUR HAPPINESS AND SUCCESS"

Family, Friends & Your Network

YvonneB

Relationships. No matter the type of relationship, be it family, intimate, friends or business connections, they form a crucial role in life. The people in your life provide support, love, encouragement and guidance; they help you to grow and be connected, they are your life collaborators and represent unity in your world.

In times of trouble, relationships are what often help you bounce back when things go wrong. For this reason, it is important to be aware of who is in your life, how the relationship operates and whether it is serving both parties in a respectful way. Often relationships can show up as being one-sided, with one person

path to making your dreams a reality. Grab the opportunity to paint a beautiful life; not a perfect one, a beautiful one.

Now, imagine waking up tomorrow and being told *'today, you are free to do as you please'*, what would you do?

Would you side step everyone else's expectations to be free? Would you risk exploring what is possible for you? Might that freedom leave you feeling expanded by life's opportunities?

All that your life is, is an accumulation of the choices you have made to date. If you have not experienced the freedom you desire, upgrade your choices, commit to taking action, and create the day, week or month you want; one day at a time.

Depression Sets In

You feel low. It's not a one-off experience, it is consistent and persistent in its company. It's not so much you don't want life to feel better, but you have become so disjointed from it, you don't know what to do, who to turn to or how to ask for help. In fact, you do your best to hide just how dark your world feels. Freedom is the farthest thing from your mind. Any day you had before this was better than this.

Depression affects mind and body. It can come and go without warning. It is a lonely place that keeps you prisoner and where life feels hopeless. You lash out at the people you love, you cancel plans last minute, you hide away and feed the pain with by drinking more; that at least gives you some respite as it numbs your thinking temporarily. This is not a turnaround point. Chronic depression is an illness; it is a chemical imbalance in the brain, you need real help and it is vital to acknowledge the need so that you can get the support required.

Create Freedom

As you look at this spiral down and the previous ones reflect on them and ask yourself; Where am I in these spirals? At what point, do I start to turn my life around so that I can truly live the life I want? What can I do to protect myself from spiralling out of control and away from freedom?

There will never be a perfect time to be free. If you can claim your freedom now, claim it. Dream your dreams, carve out your

Unhappiness Becomes the Norm

Eventually, you wake up one day and see how unhappy you are. Life has become one hard effort after another. You rarely laugh, you rarely spend time with others, no one wants to put themselves in the firing line, and whatever energy you use to have, is gone.

Your emotional health is at an all-time low and you splutter around in a never-ending cycle of sorrow, anxiousness, and stress, sometimes crying for no apparent reason. You ask yourself what's the point? You are. You are the very reason to turn things around. You are much more than this state. But if you choose to ignore change, there is always another route.

Stress; The Unfairness of Life

And you are back to impacting your health. The negative attitude turns to stress. Stress affects your body's hormone balance and depletes the brain of the chemicals required to feel happy. Longer term this can damage your immune system leaving you more susceptible to illness.

Chronic stress can lead to reducing life longevity and you must ask yourself; is this what you want in your life, this constant bleak cold detachment. It's hard to imagine anything better from here. No words of wisdom from those still around to care can break through the angry clouds encasing you. It's like watching the lights go out, one at a time.

Once here, connecting with others becomes a trial and even if you do, they are unlikely to stick around for long.

Blaming Others for Your Quality of Life, or Lack There Of

Now you turn to blaming others for what you didn't get to do, haven't got, will never achieve. You become the master of externalising, taking little if any responsibility for the state of your life.

With your blame tinted glasses firmly in place, you irrationally believe someone or something else is at fault and go all out to identify the culprit. As if that wasn't enough, as your blame escalates so does your ability to cause pain; name calling, ignoring, insulting and in the very worst-case scenario, getting angry enough to physically hurt someone.

You, take little if any responsibility. You don't see how not doing the things you wanted to have led you here. And the thought of taking off the blame tinted glasses to have a good look at yourself, the decisions you've made and your behaviour, is not an option.

Life feels empty. People do their best not to be around you and you know it. You still won't take responsibility, that would require admitting you were making bad judgement calls all along. And so, you continue to slip further down into unhappiness.

allows you to check out of the world for a while. But no big deal, you have got everything under control, right?

If ever there was a time to reassess your life, this is it. Ignore it, shrug it off and you can expect the feeling to grow. And as it grows you notice what other people have, how happy other people appear to be and you slip a little bit further down the slope.

Resentful of others having more, doing more, being more

Feeling like you do about life and then having to watch other people go about their lives seemingly in a much better place than you can be quite a painful experience. Even when it's people close to you. You know you should be happy for them, you want to celebrate their wins but quite frankly, it's not fair. You resent the happiness of others, you resent what they are achieving and inevitably resent them for having what you believe you should have or want to have.

Resentment is the persistent feeling that you are not being treated fairly. You feel undervalued, unappreciated and angry. The biggest issue with resentment is that it can lie under the surface for long periods of time, growing, brewing, waiting. Without the adrenaline rush that high levels of anger produce, it simmers instead. It becomes a way of being; a habit. It is a mood you drag yourself out of just to take a break from its grip. It affects your health and general wellbeing and it heightens your vigilance to the point where you can read something into anything and everything.

under the surface. You can't think of anything pressing to do so you do nothing; boredom arrives.

It turns out that boredom is something to be concerned with. During the 1980's a team of university researchers developed the Boredom Proness Scale (BPS) to measure how prone a person is to boredom. Referencing the scale, those who are prone to boredom are also prone to other more concerning traits that lead to stress, depression and drug addiction.

It is thought that during boredom brain activity is high in those areas where hypothetical thinking and thinking about people takes place. Just as the body requires physical activity to strengthen and tone it, so the brain requires stimulation to maintain its plasticity and flexibility. Without any stimulus, boredom sets in and that old phrase, use it or lose it, becomes very real.

Fail to notice the onset of boredom and to do something about it puts you one foot onto the slippery slope.

Dissatisfaction with life

You land in a gooey messy place called dissatisfaction. Chances are you stay stuck in your dissatisfaction because you don't know what to do about it. You know you're not the only person dealing with it, it's just another thing you must put up with.

Here's the thing, the more dissatisfied you feel, the more likely you are to start looking for something to fill the gap. Food, alcohol, relationships; anything that fills the gap, that eases the pain and

- Resentment of others having more, doing more, being more

- Blaming others for your lack of quality of life

- Unhappy on a day to day basis

- Stressed because life is unfair

- Depressed because you can't see a way out of the emotional bubble you have become trapped in

What starts off as something everyone experiences from time to time, boredom ends up in a gloomy place where hope is lost.

Right Now

You know life could be better, in fact, you would go so far as to say your life needs an upgrade. You feel uninspired by daily events even when you are in good company. It's an internal thing, like an emptiness or something is missing but you can't quite put your finger on it. In your lifetime, you may have travelled, worked in various industries, possibly even dedicated your skills and knowledge to one employer but if you were asked about your life satisfaction you would say, 'I'm not'. Change is necessary but who knows what that looks like.

Boredom Sets In

Boredom is one of those things that can creep up on you. You are, overall, okay. In fact, things are *'fine'* and fine is defined as; *Freaked out, Insecure, Neurotic, Emotional* – this is what is bubbling

- You have no idea what freedom means to you and that scares you

If you continue to think these are valid reasons not to create freedom, you will remain shackled to the humdrum life you dislike and you make yourself sick in the process.

The Downward Spiral from Not Creating Freedom

Every single day there are people living a life they hate. They wake up and go through the same old routine and tell themselves it's normal. They step onto the treadmill and join the rat race without another thought. They go through the motions of the day, complaining, bitching, blaming and unhappy. Why? Because everyone else does it. Why should they be different? Why should you?

If you are one of those people who loves their daily routine and I mean really, love it, then you are in a lucky minority; enjoy it. Most people settle for it, pretend it doesn't bother them whilst feeling chained to their routine and become resentful when they see others claiming their freedom.

Without waking up to what is possible for you, you will continue to live a joyless life. Why would you do that? By not creating the freedom you desire in your life you are likely to experience the following:

- Boredom

- Dissatisfaction with life

Creating freedom frees you to be you. What you must do is define what freedom means to you and begin to imagine living your life that way. Be free to dream.

How You Fail to Create Freedom

Imagine waking up tomorrow and being told 'today, you are free to do as you please', what would you do?

Now think about the question because the point of it is this; for most of you, you can wake up tomorrow and say to yourself I am free to do as I please… but you don't. And here's why:

- You believe you can't

- You believe you must do what is expected of you

- You believe that you must conform… everyone else does

- You choose to people please over considering your heart's desires

- You don't think you have many choices if any

- You are a wife so it's not possible

- You are a mother so it's not possible

- You don't deserve it

- You are more concerned with what other people will think than you are with creating the life you want; criticism, judgements, dislike

- Opening yourself up to challenges

- Exploring your strengths, skills, and abilities; the resources you have inside of you

- Expanding your knowledge

- Expressing who you are in the world

- Inviting abundance and prosperity into your life

Depending on where you live in the world, the level of freedom you experience each day might be outside of your control; governments, dictators, regimes that serve to keep you small; more reason, then, for those of us who have greater freedoms to maximise them. Change comes from multiple actions, small and large that create a ripple effect. In the western world, we often take for granted our freedom to dress as we like, vote, have a voice, work, study, be true to our sexuality and explore religion as we choose. Everyone should have those freedoms but they don't. In today's world, we still have women living as second class citizens and not free, an injustice we must all work together to overcome.

"By claiming your freedom, you can help others claim theirs"

Creating freedom gives you the flexibility required to design the way you want to live your life in the knowledge you can have the lifestyle you want if you are prepared to do the work.

CHAPTER 6
Creating Freedom

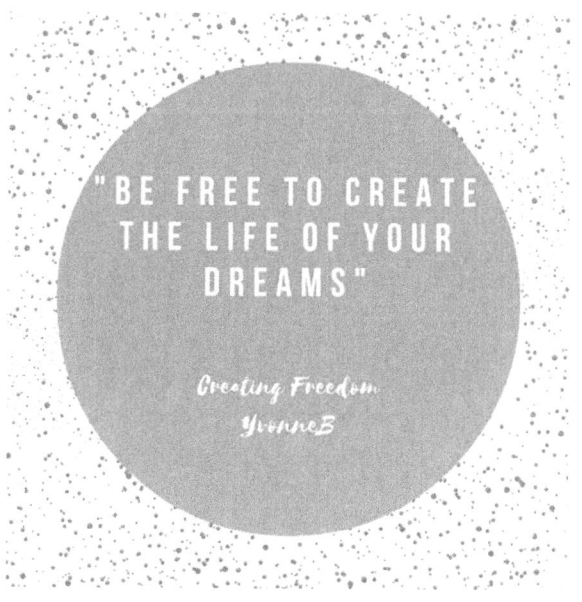

Creating freedom is about claiming your space on the planet. It is about letting go of the fears that hamper you; pain, resentment, rejection, being wrong, failing, people, the past, the future, limiting beliefs; and making decisions on who, what, where and how you want to live your life.

When you decide to create freedom in your life you are:

- Discovering what is possible for you

- Stepping into the unknown

- Opening yourself up to risk

- Embracing your vulnerability

even know it. The light that once shone brightly with ideas, thoughts, and possibilities, has faded away.

The Healthy Side of Fear

Living fearlessly frees you from the chains of living life others design for you.

Remember there will always be fear, you are wired for it but that wiring is there to support you in life-saving situations; for survival. It is not there to prevent you exploring the possibilities or to keep you small, wishing you could do more, be more, have more; you can.

Getting your mindset right is a necessary step to managing your fears. When you can think through fearful situations with clarity and understanding and be aware of the feelings fear brings up, you are better placed to manage and leverage those feelings.

The healthy side of fear requires taking the time to understand how you operate from a primitive to a logical level, accepting fear exists for a reason whilst enabling yourself to control it as opposed to it controlling you.

You Are Miserable

Fed up, drained and caught in a cycle of excuses and blame, you realise how allowing your fear to lead you has made you a prisoner. Happiness is a fleeting feeling, unsustainable for any notable length of time and you are lacklustre. You know that life is not meant to feel this way but you have lost all sense of purpose and struggle to see how or why you deserve anything more than what is your current reality and you don't feel grateful for that either. You wish you had a plan to change things but who has the energy or time for that?

Your Life Is Not in Your Hands

You wake up some days and wonder who you are. Who is this person you have become? You get up and go through the motions of daily life, avoiding anything that challenges you, allowing life to push and pull you at will. It might be your life but you have no control over it. Life has become a force that dictates to you; you just listen and react as required. You are a shell of your former self, your dreams and hopes have long since departed.

Responsibility Is a Thing of The Past

Why take responsibility for something you are unable to control? You live in the shadows of your life being a fraction of who you are just to get by. Your confidence is shredded, you accept others words without a second thought and you now accept that dreams are for children, not adults. Fear is so much a part of your life you barely notice it as fear; it has become you and you don't

you feel a pang of guilt because you know the underlying reason is fear. But if no one else knows, it's okay. After all, you're not the only one not living the life they desire, you're not the only one who has put their dreams on the shelf for when the time is right... right?

Wrong. You are not someone else and your life wasn't created so that you could live in the shadows. Right here you can deal with your fears and get on track to being the victor. It's one decision away.

But making decisions is just another obstacle. If you do that, then you must follow through, there is no way out. You're just not ready, you need time to think things through and so you buy time by avoiding decisions. It doesn't feel good but at least it's not scary.

It's Your Fault

You're still not ready to deal with your fear yet but your excuses and lack of decision making have been noticed and people are beginning to challenge you. You are questioned by friends and other people in your network why you haven't done this, why you haven't been there and it's uncomfortable. Now it's time to turn that fear outward and blame someone else. If it's not the demanding kids and partner, it's your uncaring boss. In fact, it is anyone but you. Now you have dragged other people into the equation and it's difficult to U-turn your way back on track because if you do, you will be caught in a lie; and no one likes a liar.

- Impairs formation of long-term memories

- Leaves you making excuses and avoiding making decisions

- Allows you to always find someone else to blame

- Means you struggle to maintain any level of happiness and feel emotionally drained

- Leaves you feeling out of control; external locus of control

- Ends with you struggling to take responsibility for your life

Right Now

You think about all the things you would love to do; the places you want to visit, the people you want to meet, the kind of work you imagine pouring yourself into. Yes, you think a lot. But every time you get an image in your mind of just how great life could be something stops you in your tracks. Sometimes it feels like an invisible wall preventing you from moving forwards and other times it's the voice inside your head, the one warning you of the dangers of your dreams. The voice that asks you 'Who the hell are you?' or the one that whispers softly how much you have in your past to hide and so it is better to stay small, quiet and in the background.

Excuses, Excuses, Decisions, Decisions

You're busy, always busy, far too busy in fact to do the things you say you want to do. There's work, the kids, the partner, the in-laws; there is everything but time. But for every excuse you make,

Fear from Your Past

You have shut the door on the skeletons in your cupboard and are so busy holding it shut, you miss out on living. You fear the truth yet you want truth in your life. You fear judgement but you want to live a judgement free life. In the end, you accept others' bad behaviours because you have a guilty mind, a guilty heart and underneath it all, you feel worthless, undeserving of anything better.

Fear of the Future

New situations, new chapters in life cause you to retreat into yourself. Change looms overhead and you fight to stay where you are. But change is necessary and the more you fight it the worse it feels. You become exhausted, stressed and empty of energy, clinging onto sameness as if your life depended on it.

It's time to stop avoiding life and start living it. Breaking free of these fears will allow you to discover who you are at your very core and give you the freedom to shape you into your best self.

Allowing Fear to Rule You Is Not the Answer to A Better You

The impact of fear is deeper than you think. It:

- Activates your amygdala, which plays a key role in the way you process emotions

- Weakens your immune system

How You Never Win with Fear

Fear of Failure

When you begin to believe that failure is everything you don't get right, you limit your potential. You stop striving to do things outside of your comfort zone. You refuse to expand and explore what is possible for you.

Fear of Rejection

When you take 'no' as a personal rejection, you are making it personal instead of seeing it as a rejection to an event or situation the responding person is not ready for. And you begin to close down your feelings to keep yourself safe. You live, but only giving part of you, never all of you... just in case. Being part of you is not being your best self and therefore impedes you living your best life.

Fear of Being Wrong

When you say something and others disagree, whether mildly or severely, and you stop sharing your thoughts and opinions for fear of being ridiculed or being wrong, you lose your voice, your sense of who you are and stop being you.

Fear of Letting People Down

When you constantly seek to people please for an easy life or to be liked; you avoid negative judgement as part of your daily routine. Your every act comes from a place of fear and you are no longer you. Other people shape you and mould you to their will because you allow them to.

others expectations, meeting others needs that you have spent little if any time considering your own needs and possibilities.

See Fear for What It Is

Apart from real fear, the type that gets you moving to save your life like a fire or falling from a great height, begin to see fear for what it is:

- **F**alse

- **E**xpectations

- **A**ppearing

- **R**eal

Most of your fears are pre-event visualisations of the worst outcome. They appear real because you project the worst possible outcome and anchor strong emotions to that outcome; feelings of failure, embarrassment, being a laughing stock, being disliked, being irresponsible and not meeting other people's expectations.

One of the most common fears is the fear of failure. But what does it mean? At what point, do you fail? When you don't get something right or when you don't get back up and try again? These are questions to ask yourself if fear is hindering you from doing the things in your heart and stopping you from living the life you desire.

respond to situations as if we were still under the threat our ancestors faced.

How often have you watched some thrill seeker scaling buildings, jumping off cliffs, running over rooftops and thought 'they are crazy'. Are they fear free or have they accepted that fear is an emotion that is within their control? Or are they indeed crazy?

It is important to develop a sense of fearlessness if you want to be your best self because uncontrolled fear will cripple you. It will hold you back and keep you small. It will scream no when you want to say yes. As the famous quote goes *'whether you think you can or you can't, you're right'* (Henry Ford). Being fearless allows you to surrender.

Stripping away the fears that have been taught, such as those developed through expectations of others, judgements of others, not being liked, failure, success - as it leads to higher expectation - not being enough, past mistakes and many phobias, will set you free to be your best you.

Building the mindset of a victor, not a victim; someone who refuses to be limited by fear even when fear feels present is the aim. As the victim, you say *'it's impossible'* but as the victor, you say *'I am possible'*. As the victim, you believe you will fail, but as the victor, you choose to believe you can and will succeed. It's a mindset.

And even as you contemplate your mindset be aware of enemy number one; You. You are likely to be your biggest critic. Why? Because so much of your time will have been spent trying to satisfy

CHAPTER 5

Being Fearless

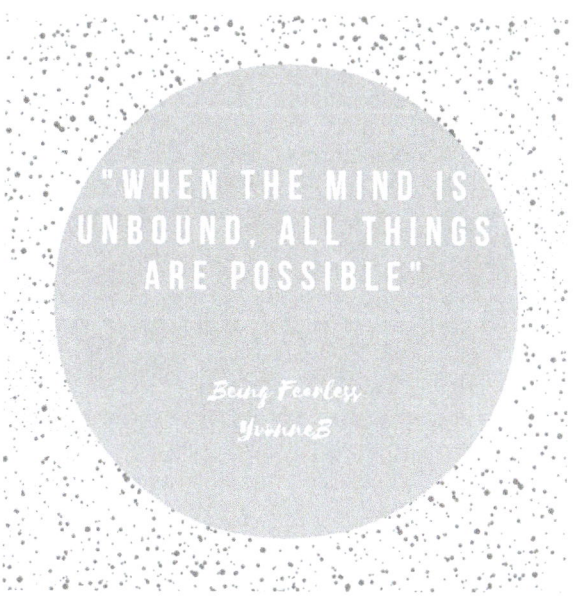

"WHEN THE MIND IS UNBOUND, ALL THINGS ARE POSSIBLE"

Being Fearless
YvonneB

What does it mean to be fearless? Is being fearless the same as never feeling fear again?

Being fearless is the ability to manage fear in otherwise fearful situations. Notice the key word here; manage. It does not mean that fear has gone forever, it does not mean that all sense of fight or flight has dissipated nor would you want it to. Your brain is wired to detect situations that threaten your survival and that is a good thing.

I believe that most fears are learned. It's been said that we are only born with two fears; the fear of falling and the fear of loud noises, although I would add to that the fear of pain. What is clear is that we act out of fear based on out of date mental software. We

With a healthy mind, you manage the day to day challenges with confidence and awareness. Your ability to maintain good relationships with others means you are far less likely to feel or be cut off; left feeling lonely and alone.

The healthy mind is engaged with the world, adapting and managing the changes and uncertainties of life.

If you have been under the illusion that mind issues will only appear later in life or only if you have a traumatic event to deal with, think again. Every day people are suffering from mental illness caused by, or that have been contributed to, changing jobs, divorce, feelings of inadequacy, poor nutrition, substance abuse, infections, and genetics.

Being Fit & Healthy Is Less of An Option, More of A Rule

At the end of the day, only you can decide what is truly important to you, what you are prepared to do to optimize your quality of life and what you believe is necessary to achieve being your best. But without being fit and healthy just how much quality do you expect to get?

Being fit and healthy is not a dress size, body shape, gym membership or having to be a fitness freak. Being fit and healthy is a move away from feelings of not being enough, low self-esteem, poor self-image, stress and all its connected symptoms.

Being your best begins with you taking care of you. No excuses, no blame.

in turn, take you further into a state of hopelessness. You reach a breaking point.

The Bottom of the Slippery Slope

At the bottom of this slippery slope you are likely to feel so cut off from the rest of the world, a way out seems neither visible or possible.

Here you are faced with the possibilities of mild cognitive impairment, forgetting important information you would once have recalled at the drop of a hat; conversations, recent events. If diagnosed with MCI, you have an increased risk of developing Alzheimer's or other types of dementia.

How quickly one can shift through these phases on the way down will vary depending on the person and the circumstances that set the spiral in motion. But it is critical to be aware that no one sets out to become stressed, depressed or suffering from MCI. Your ability to be aware of your feelings and your thoughts will help you identify when things are not as they should be and the sooner you get help, the better. The sooner you make a change the better.

The Healthy Mind

Whether you think you are already in this spiral or just think it is possible for you, it is important to reach out to someone you trust. And now is the time, not tomorrow, not next week.

straight or to make sense of things, sometimes everyday things. Without an outlet for the stress it can:

- Interfere with your judgement, causing you to make bad decisions

- Affect your ability to stay focused

- Increase the stress hormone, cortisol, affecting brain functions that lead to mood disorders or other mental issues. When there are excessive amounts of cortisol in the system it can lead to weight gain, heart disease, diabetes and hormone imbalances amongst other things

Memory Over and Out

When there is too much pressure, systems tend to shut down. The body does it and so does the mind. At this point, you find it difficult to stay focused on things for any length of time. You feel tired, exhausted and your moods can change in a heartbeat. Then your sleep pattern no longer exists and you catch sleep as and when you can.

More pressure, more shut down. Retaining information in a mind already on overload and in a tired state is difficult. You begin neglecting important things in your life; work performance, your home, your relationships and your personal appearance.

You become more and more detached from real world thinking with irrational thoughts becoming more common. You turn to food, alcohol, cigarettes and drugs hoping for some peace but they,

it thinks best fits the situation, with survival and reproduction as its top priorities, and the emotion felt is used to influence the rest of the body to react accordingly. Using the dog scenario, if the brain evaluates it is an aggressive dog, the emotions you feel will put you into fight or flight mode and your survival instincts will kick in; for most of us, that means to run and scream.

Imagine then that your mind is not being well looked after; poor nutrition, lack of challenging stimuli, lack of new ways of seeing things. Your mind will react in the only ways it knows how; how you have trained it to over the years, good or bad. Now think about that in relation to your fears. When you are unable to manage your emotions, they take over. They feel bigger than you and that feels scary.

Handling Stress

If you are unable to manage your emotion's it adds up that you will struggle to deal with stress. Any situation that brings discomfort is likely to push you to the edge. Things will look bleaker than they are, they will feel worse than they are and before you know it, you will only be able to think, feel and see the worst. Your stress levels will rise and your ability to think straight will decrease.

When Nothing Makes Sense

As with so many of today's health issues, stress overwhelms and exhausts you. In this state, it becomes very difficult to think

Right Now

You might be thinking about learning new things, expanding your knowledge and fine tuning your mental agility. Unfortunately, your 'thinking' and 'doing' are not aligned. Instead of picking up a good book you switch on the T.V. Instead of watching a programme that expands your knowledge, you get sucked into the latest soap; day in, day out. It seems harmless enough and after a hard day's work, it feels like a treat. You deserve the down time. Over time where does that lead to?

Striking A Balance

Downtime is important and how you spend it is up to you. However, do not fool yourself into thinking you are striking a balance; work all day equates to watching reality T.V. shows all night. Your brain has the capacity to grow, strengthening and creating new neural pathways, where neurons, or nerve cells, travel to transport information; by changing routine and doing things differently new pathways can be created. Doing the same old thing in the same old way reinforces current habits; no change required. And soon enough that habit becomes a way of life and what I refer to as living on constant autopilot; no thinking required.

You Think, You Feel, You React

Your emotions are not just what you feel. They are made up of thoughts, feelings, and reactions. For example, you might see a dog and your brain evaluates what is being seen; friendly dog or aggressive dog. The brain then creates an emotional response that

people, places, the media, and so many other feeds. Without taking responsibility for what **you** input into your mind, you can guarantee your thoughts, your ability to challenge through questioning and your decision-making will be based on information others have given or poured into you; with no questions asked. Even worse, your ability to think and make decisions deteriorates.

The Downward Spiral of the Mind

Looking after your mind, just like looking after your body, is essential to being your best self. Per a 2012 study carried out by University College London, it found that brain function declined by 3.6% between the ages of 45-49 (the test sample included 7000 people working in civil service roles between 1997-2007 and the mental tests were given at the start and end of the study). And other research has shown similar as well as much earlier signs of decline.

Failing to look after and nurture the mind can lead to many of the same outcomes already mentioned for the body but here are a few others to be aware of:

- The ability to manage your emotions

- Handling stress

- The ability to reason

- Memory & attention span issues

- Cognitive Impairment

Just as the body can go down a slippery slope so too can the mind. We live in an age where mental illness is on the rise. For those of you who have not experienced it, you might be inclined to assume it is something you can bypass, it will never happen to you. But you better wake up out of that slumber because:

- One in four people in the world will be affected by mental or neurological disorders at some point in their lives

- Around 450 million people currently suffer from such conditions, placing mental disorders among the leading causes of ill-health and disability worldwide

- Treatments are available, but nearly two-thirds of people with a known mental disorder never seek help from a health professional

- Stigma, discrimination, and neglect prevent care and treatment from reaching people with mental disorders, says the World Health Organization

Good mental wellbeing enables you to develop your potential, to think clearly, creatively and decisively. It also impacts the way you connect with people.

Mental wellbeing encapsulates how you are feeling and how well you are coping with day-to-day life.

How You Fail Your Mind

Simply put, if you do not look after your mind someone or something else will. You are influenced every day by words,

The Healthy Body

Now is the time to reconnect by taking care of yourself first. Just as you put your own drop down face mask on during a flight in trouble, so you must put your health first to better help and serve others.

You may have been sold a story of how boring good health is; you can't eat this, don't drink that, you should exercise 30 minutes every day... on and on the list, goes. But taking care of your health has nothing to do with these imposed limitations. Taking care of your health is about respecting yourself. It's about loving you and knowing you deserve the best so that you can be your best.

I can tell you from personal experience that the best things you can do for your health are the things that leave you feeling energized, mobile, active and content with your self-image.

Stuff perfection, stuff limitations, start making meaningful choices for your health and go all in.

Your Mind; The Driver

As I mentioned before, true health is the combined wellbeing of body and mind; they are intrinsically linked and are at the core of being your best you, leading to you living your best life.

You are wired from birth to take in the earliest messages for translation, be they good or bad. If you don't stop to check those messages and what they mean to you, you will be as influenced by the bad ones as you are the good ones.

Illnesses

Ultimately your health slips through your fingers and the worst outcome becomes your reality. You can't even remember how you got here, your body suffering, your mind not functioning. But here you are. Illness becomes part and parcel of your daily life and you live with it. You long for those days when things were better when you felt better.

The Bottom of the Slippery Slope

This is how easy it is to lose sight of what is important. You need only take your eye off the prize of good health for a short while and before you know it, your life has changed forever.

This is when physical activity stops being a choice and starts being your life saver.

My question to you then is this; How far down the slippery slope do you need to go before you see sense? Do you have to hit rock bottom with no alternative but to change or do you dare to tackle it right now when things are not anywhere near that life threatening? You see, when you understand the value of your health, in fact, your life counts on it, and you constantly and consistently put it first, you learn how to avoid the habits and actions that do not serve you well. In peak health, you learn how to deal with life's challenges head on.

can diffuse the rush, the chemicals will find another way out causing headaches, indigestion, nausea.

Is it any wonder then that your emotions go haywire? It's like turning up the volume on the radio; from stress to **distress**; pure negative stress, into **anxiousness**; worry, nervousness, unease and ending up in the murky fear filled world of **depression**.

Depression

Per a study published in PLOS Medicine, depression is the second leading cause of disability across the globe. In fact, slightly more than 4% of the global population are diagnosed with the disorder.

Depression, at this level, leaves you feeling helpless, hopeless and worthless. You would get up and face the world if you could think of one good reason to do so but that reason fails you. Functioning on a day to day basis feels worse than trying to pull yourself out of a large pool of quicksand. Here, the effort, energy and focus to make change is a whole other scenario and it will take great support, love and internal determination to make the shift, but the shift can be made.

From here your health can be used as the rope that pulls you up or the slide that takes you down. And even at this stage, when no light at the end of the tunnel can be seen, you still have a choice. A harder one, yes, but a choice remains.

You breathe approximately 18 times per minute, 1,080 times an hour and 25,920 times a day and it's likely you don't give it a second thought. Yet when your health takes a downturn, breathing difficulties might be a sign that things are getting out of hand. In fact, ineffective breathing is connected to:

- Health issues such as asthma and high blood pressure

- Stress

- Digestion

- Panic attacks, insomnia and extreme fatigue

Still not ready to change? Let's go down another level.

Stress

You have heard it many times, not all stress is bad for you. A little bit of stress can go a long way in the right situation but consistent daily stress that turns into chronic stress, can kill you; no exaggeration, no jokes.

By now your stress has probably been building and if you are aware enough of the stress, be it about your health, finances, relationship or any other area of your life, you know it MUST be dealt with. That constant feeling of being under threat, out of control, operating in the fight or flight state where adrenaline and noradrenaline chemicals kick in, increases your blood pressure, your heart rate and level of perspiration. The chemicals need to go somewhere and if you are not in a real fight situation where you

Drained; Where Has All Your Energy Gone?

You want to get off this downward spiral but quite frankly you have barely got enough energy to care. You try to eat well for a few days but nothing changes. You think about exercising but that exhausts you. You are currently operating on empty and there is not an energy source in sight; lethargy becomes your new best friend.

It's no longer just about your energy, now it's your enthusiasm too; there isn't any. You feel awful, and you start to think about how you use to feel, how you use to look, how much happier you were even though life was not perfect. This is one of the breakthrough moments, when you get to realise enough is enough. Why did you stop going to the gym? Why did you start eating crappy food? Why did you think it was okay to drink and smoke the days away?

Start making the changes now and you avoid the worst. Decide not to and get ready for the worst times to come.

Simple Things Like Breathing Become an Issue

Breathing is this thing you wake up doing and it probably never gets your attention until you need to exert yourself or you feel as if you can't breathe. In that moment, you struggle to take in oxygen, feeling a little out of control and you focus on catching your breath. It takes a while, you recover and breathing stops being noticed again.

goes on. And whilst these are not to be dismissed lightly, it comes back to you.

What matters more than all the above is your own desire to challenge these experiences, to detach the emotion that anchors you to them as a victim so that you can embrace your self-image from a place of love and be the victor. You are not the sum of other people's behaviours; you are not the same as other people and therefore should not compare so actively; nor are you the limits of your beliefs.

The lack of Sleep is Killing You

With all the mounting health issues, overactive thinking kicks in. It is spurred on by every ache and pain, every concern about your health, your work; heck, life! Now you're faced with sleepless nights. Every problem playing and replaying itself out until you learn to get by on 3 or 4 hours of sleep. You now force yourself through the day. You know people are noticing but they say nothing and you pretend everything is okay.

Red Alert! Sleep is as important as nutrition and exercise. It is a time for the body to repair, heal and develop. Lack of sleep affects your mood, your ability to function; and think about the implications of that when driving, cooking, or handling machinery, and very likely, your relationships. You are too tired to socialise, too tired to play with the kids, and way too tired to be intimate with your partner. And the spiral deepens.

Skin is the largest organ of the body with an approximate total area of 20 square feet; that's a vast amount of skin. It protects you from the elements and regulates your body temperature. It requires care to function and by care, I mean good nutrition and physical activity.

Without the right care, skin can become dull, washed out and dry, not to mention the added adverse effects from too much sun exposure, smoking, and alcohol all of which go on to affect self-image.

It's easy to blame skin changes on aging but the reality is, lifestyle plays a big part.

Your Self-Image Goes Out the Window

As your inner resources deplete from lack of care and use, so too does your external appearance demise. When you stop liking the person in the mirror, something must change.

A poor self-image is rarely born out of one moment. It is likely to come from an accumulation of experiences that lead you to believe you are not enough. From childhood experiences through to adult relationships, glamorized media 'how you should look' ads as well as your own personal desires, can make or break your self-image.

There are so many places to point the finger of blame here; neglect, abuse, bullying, peer pressure, manipulative relationships, persistent stress, traumatic events, media, food industry; the list

You Struggle to Move About with the Same Quality of Freedom

You may already know what it feels like to have stiff achy joints, to struggle to stretch your arm straight up above your head or to bend and touch the floor. Mobility gives us the freedom to move around with ease and it plays a significant role in healthy aging. Unless you want to become dependent on others as you advance in age, your ability to stay mobile is not a 'something to worry about later' option, it's a prevention is better than cure option. Now is as good a time as any to do something for your health.

You Find Yourself Having More Aches and Pains

When you begin to lose mobility, you tend to avoid physical activity because it hurts and the more you avoid physical activity, the more you 'feel it' when you do have to be active. Before you know it, you have more aches and pains than you can name and this doesn't only happen in old age.

Ultimately these symptoms affect your confidence and self-image. You become overly aware of your posture not being quite so upright, or the need to sit down after 10 minutes because standing makes you ache. The truth is you *feel* old, making you unhappier, more anxious and possibly more stressed.

With All the Discomfort, You Begin to Care Less

As if all the internal and external pains weren't enough, your unhealthy lifestyle begins to take the shine and health out of your skin.

- Smoking is a leading cause of cancer and death from cancer

- Smoking causes heart disease, stroke, aortic aneurysm, chronic obstructive pulmonary disease (COPD), diabetes, osteoporosis, rheumatoid arthritis, age-related macular degeneration, and cataracts, and worsens asthma symptoms in adults

- Smokers are at higher risk of developing pneumonia, tuberculosis, and other airway infections

These statistics should concern you; as human beings, as sisters, brothers, daughters, sons, as mothers and fathers.

Again; physical activity does not equal the gym. Being physically active is about moving regularly and this movement increases your wellbeing, life expectancy, builds stronger bones & muscles, aid sleep and decreases the chances of becoming depressed. These are all key factors in having a great life, experiencing the greatness of life and being your best you.

Physical activity is not some sort of punishment for overeating, for being lazy or whatever other reasons you are being told to 'get active'. It is as normal as breathing and just as needed. And the proof of that is easy to see. When you become inactive, what happens? Your health goes downhill.

We have shifted from hunter-gatherer to couch potato, and it's not pretty…

- Nearly 40 percent of the world's adults fall into fat or obese categories

- Researchers estimate that excess weight caused 3.4 million deaths worldwide in 2010

- Globally, almost one-third of adults don't get the recommended level of physical activity, per research published in 2012

- In 2012, 3.3 million deaths, or 5.9 percent of all global deaths (7.6 percent for men and 4.0 percent for women), were attributable to alcohol consumption

- Alcohol contributes to over 200 diseases and injury-related health conditions, most notably alcohol dependence, liver cirrhosis, cancers, and injuries

- In 2012, 5.1 percent of the burden of disease and injury worldwide (139 million disability-adjusted-life-years) was attributable to alcohol consumption

- Globally, alcohol misuse is the fifth leading risk factor for premature death and disability; among people between the ages of 15 and 49, it is the first

- Of the more than 7,000 chemicals in tobacco smoke, at least 250 are known to be harmful

- Smoking has been found to harm nearly every bodily organ and organ system in the body and diminishes a person's overall health

not perfect, but I get it right often enough; and for a 51-year 'young' woman, that matters. I want to be around when my son decides to get married and have children; if he does of course.

I want to take you down the spiral of health, I want you to identify where you are right now and decide if you are willing to make changes today to avoid going down the spiral one more step. Sometimes you need to see things laid out to appreciate the need for change because they aren't always obvious.

Right Now

Right now, you are living your life. You may not be overjoyed by it, you feel something is missing and you have moments, days even, of wondering what the point is; why are you are. You wonder but you do nothing about it.

You Do Less Because You Feel Tired, Uncomfortable, and it Hurts

The more fed up you become and do nothing about it, the more inactive you become. Yes, you get up and go to work, you drag yourself to the gym or fitness class once per week, you might even make the effort to go for a drink with friends at the weekend but, often, you feel too tired to do anything.

You eat more; it's comforting. You drink more; it's relaxing. You smoke more; it calms your stress... or so you tell yourself.

Well wake up to the facts of that lifestyle

- Lack of physical strength

- Poor mobility

- Aches and pains

- Tired looking skin

- Poor self-image

- Lack of sleep

- Low energy

- Lethargy

- Breathing issues

- Feelings of stress

- Distress

- Anxiousness

- Depression

- Illnesses

And the Overall impact: Disease, shortened life span

I don't tell you these things to make you feel bad or to increase your fear, I share them with you so that you can make decisions that help you, not hinder you.

The only reason I have staved off signs of aging is through my wellbeing lifestyle. I don't always get it right, my routine is certainly

Yet your health and fitness relate to the quality of life you have, your aspirations, unlocking potential, self-knowledge, self-awareness, talents, human capital, dreams, and your identity; the very things you require to be at your best.

And if you fail to put your health and fitness first, then what?

Your Body; The Temple

Your body is a precious resource you have FOR FREE! It is this amazing structure that can do amazing things when looked after and loved. Now, if quality maintenance is required to keep it in peak state why is it a battle to invest in it? A new handbag, new shoes, a new coat; no problem. But upgrade your food quality? I don't think so! This is the messy thinking we are dealing with today. It doesn't make sense but it has become the norm.

How You Fail Your Body

When you have the choice to do the best for your health and fitness yet choose not to, you dishonour yourself. And when you dishonour yourself, you take for granted and abuse key inbuilt resources that inevitably lead you to the victim state.

Your Inbuilt Resources – Abuse Them at Your Own Peril

I want to drive home to you that there is no time like the present to make changes in your wellbeing lifestyle. Failing to do so may lead to:

I know, You Know

You might be thinking 'I KNOW this stuff', there is nothing new here but if you are not doing anything about it, what good is the knowledge serving? What is it going to take to get you to move from knowing to doing? How far do you need to spiral down to climb back up?

5 A Day for Your Body	5 A Day for Your Mind
Health Education	Personal Development
Nutrition	Nutrition
Exercise	Exercise
Physical Challenges	Mental Challenges
Rest	Rest

It might be that you are lacking purpose, that things have become so challenging in your life you struggle to see how being fit and healthy is going to make a difference. You might even believe that the whole health and fitness industry is a fad, full of money making schemes and products that play on vulnerable people.

Think about the professional athlete; they have the mental and physical strength to do things that haven't been done before, to set new world records, to train for hours on end. Why? Because they look after their mind and bodies. I am sure there are top athletes who eat junk food but they work out 4-8 hours per day. They burn off more calories in a day than most people do in a week, or even in a month. Their energy balance is likely to be in deficit when they are in training season; more calories burnt up than taken in. Yet they still ensure their diet is balanced with good quality nutrients because the body needs them.

Sadly, we live in a time of excess. There is an endless supply of food choices 24/7 and you don't even have to go and shop for it; it is brought to your door. People are eating more, moving less. Food is being 'designed' today packed with ingredients that rob good health so is it any wonder we have such high obesity rates, mental health issues, increased preventable death rates?

I don't want to get too bleak but this one principle alone can change your life forever. If you choose to make the change of having a healthier lifestyle, your quality of life will alter, how you see life will alter and how you experience life will change.

In the world of wellbeing your '5 a day' is not an endless list of fruit and vegetables, it consists of the 5 MUST focus points for optimal health, increased energy and wellbeing.

CHAPTER 4
Being Fit & Healthy

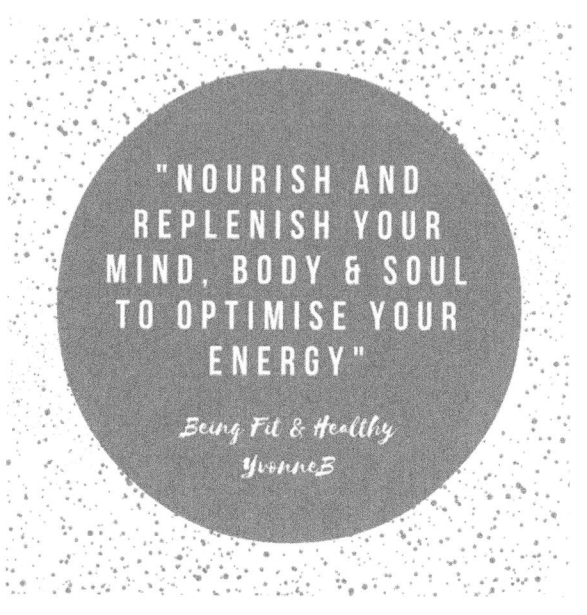

"NOURISH AND REPLENISH YOUR MIND, BODY & SOUL TO OPTIMISE YOUR ENERGY"

Being Fit & Healthy
YvonneB

Let's get crystal clear, being fit and healthy is not about going on a diet and heading to the gym. It is not a certain dress size. Being fit and healthy is about understanding the importance of how you can generate enough energy to provide the strength and vitality required to sustain your physical and mental wellbeing.

Healthy eating, for example, is not about dieting, it is about getting the right energy, calories, from the right types of food - as clean and unprocessed and chemically untampered with as possible - to give your body what it needs to function so that it can work and communicate with your brain for mental health. Mental and physical health are intrinsically linked and you must respect them if you truly want to be your best.

- Having faith in God, self and the universal laws that knowingly want the best for us: living life fully without fear – Faith

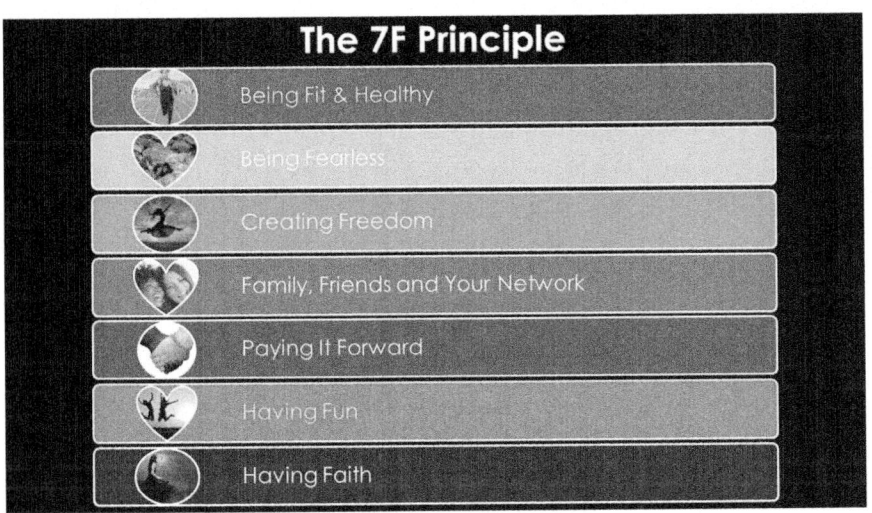

What If...

Think about it; How different do you think your life would be if you made improvements in one or more of these areas of your life?

And as importantly, what happens if you don't make any changes at all?

I want to show you the potential spirals, as they connect to the 7F Principles, you could find yourself going down towards poor health and an unfulfilling fruitless life. You might be on one already and if you are, it's time for change...

CHAPTER 3
Enter The 7F Principle

And that's where the 7F principles come in. They are simple principles to implement so that you can begin removing the shackles of the victim and free yourself to be the victor; the best version of you. They ensure your needs are being met at all levels of development. They work from the inside out because everything begins at the core of YOU and everything is connected.

What are these 7F Principles?

- Being fit & healthy by looking after your wellbeing: secure, stable, sound – Survival

- Being fearless by freeing your mind from limiting beliefs, judgements and expectations: stimulated, stirred, searching - Experience

- Creating freedom as defined by you: exploring, expanding, expressing self - Discovery

- Surrounding yourself with loving family, friends and a network of like-minded people: authentic, assertive, aware, companionship, community, caring – Love

- Paying it forward to create a ripple effect of being the best you can be: contributing, creating, connecting - Serve

- Having fun in your life raising your vibration: energy, excitement, enjoyment – Joyful Expression

- Exposing the skeletons in your closet so that you can break the chains of guilt, stress, and shame – you are not an event, you are not your past behaviours

- Letting go of the limitations that have been whispered to you over the years so that you can experience freedom as defined by you

- Deciding that enough is enough and being disciplined with yourself as you begin new ways of being

- Being vulnerable and knowing it is not a sign of weakness but of true inner strength

- Taking that leap of faith into a new way of being, believing life is an amazing gift

What Is Being Your Best You?

Being your best you, has nothing to do with perfection, having a problem free life, an easy ride, being right, being better than others. It's about:

- Being open to the challenges you face knowing they will make you more of who you are

- Being authentic, knowing who you are without apology – not everyone will like you but that is not your problem

- Being loving – connected to people, community, the world, the planet

- Knowing you are enough and no failure or experience can take that away unless you allow it to

- Searching out the lessons from the life experiences that show up to challenge you; the pain, betrayals, hate, anger, failure

- Never settling and falling into complacency

- Feeling the fear and screwing it over; looking fear in the eye and making sure it turns away before you do

- Raising your energy, your vibration to operate from your highest self

- Taking ownership and responsibility for the life you want to live

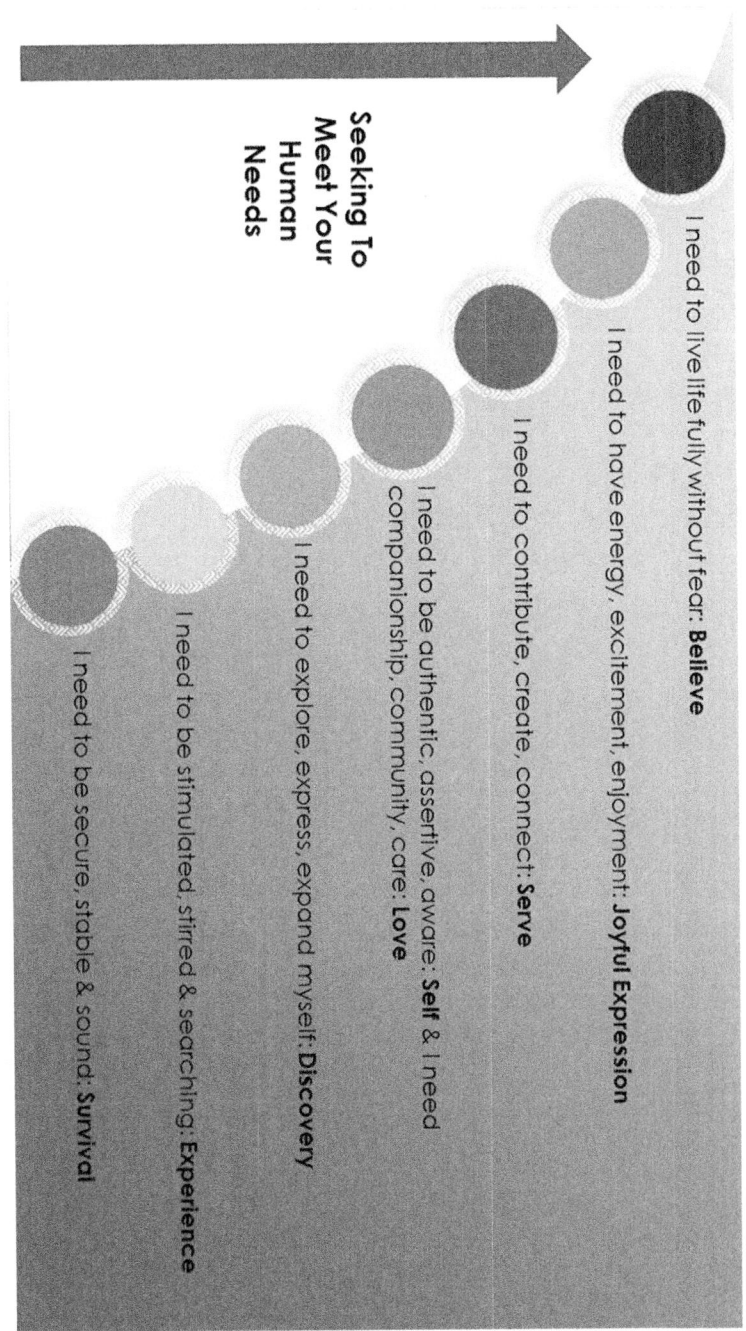

MEETING YOUR HUMAN NEEDS

Seeking To Meet Your Human Needs

- I need to live life fully without fear: **Believe**
- I need to have energy, excitement, enjoyment: **Joyful Expression**
- I need to contribute, create, connect: **Serve**
- I need to be authentic, assertive, aware: **Self** & I need companionship, community, care: **Love**
- I need to explore, express, expand myself: **Discovery**
- I need to be stimulated, stirred & searching: **Experience**
- I need to be secure, stable & sound: **Survival**

There Comes a Turning Point

- What did you do or say to someone else to make you think you don't deserve better?
- What skeletons do you have in your closet?
- What way of life has caused you to experience pain?
- Where do your feelings of guilt come from?
- What makes you think you aren't enough?
- Why don't you deserve the best?
- What is the worst or biggest lie you have ever told?
- Who haven't you forgiven?
- Which One of Your Human Needs Isn't Being Met?

By answering these questions honestly and taking responsibility for your part in the outcomes of your life, you can begin to free yourself from the burden they are currently placing on you.

You MUST go back to the moments that closed you down to let go of them. You MUST reframe what they mean to you; instead of identifying as the victim of an event, look for the lesson and be the victor; choose to overcome. This must be a conscious decision that you embed into yourself. This requires you to forgive, to confront, to release emotions, to realise 'it' was then and now is now. Easy? Probably not but ask yourself:

'Ask Yourself' Exercise

- How important is it for you to move forward?

- How important is it for you to live a richer life?

- How much do you want to know what is possible for you?

- What are you willing to do to have your best life yet?

- What will happen if you don't start living your best life now?

- Who have you been trying to please?

- Whose standards have you been trying to live up to?

- What or who led you to believe what you believe about yourself?

- What has caused you to lose hope in life?

- When were you at your lowest?

CHAPTER 2
There Comes a Turning Point

Just like the caterpillar that turns into a butterfly, your life challenges are an opportunity to metamorphosis into your greater self. You MUST go through these things, however undesired, to realise you are phenomenal. This is not about what is fair because who said life was fair?

The biggest challenge you face is that often you lose hope before the change comes and get stuck in a rut of despair, failure, loss, and hate. You believe that life is meant to be straightforward, problem-free, free from failure if you follow the rules laid out for you. You strive to meet others expectations, you create habits, behaviours, and stories that prevent you from having the life you want; and excuses make the pain go away... temporarily.

But this is not a lesson in blame either. It is not your fault if you find yourself in a rut. You have been conditioned through your experiences to build a solid wall around you, to protect yourself as best you can, to shield yourself from further pain.

And when you have tried to deal with the prison you have locked yourself in you have been bombarded with messages to think positive thoughts, act like you are already there, be thankful for what you have, just be happy. And these are important things to do, granted, but the truth is...

What's Wrong with Your Life?

Why me?	What can I learn?
I can't	I can
It's their fault	It's my responsibility
Things couldn't be any worse	Something good will come from this
What if it gets worse?	What if it gets better?
I've failed	I've learned something
I hate life	I embrace life
I have endless problems	There are solutions to my problems
Ungrateful	Grateful
Self-absorbed	Compassionate
Hateful conversations	Loving conversations
Expects the worst	Expects the best
Lacks belief in self and others	Has faith in self and others
Lacks awareness of their behaviour	Emotionally intelligent
Constantly makes excuses	Takes ownership
Talks about change	Makes changes
Constantly feels drained	Feels energized
Feels disconnected from their world	Feels connected to their world
Can see no way out	Seeks for the way out
Imprisoned	Free
Refuses to believe change is possible	Takes a leap of faith

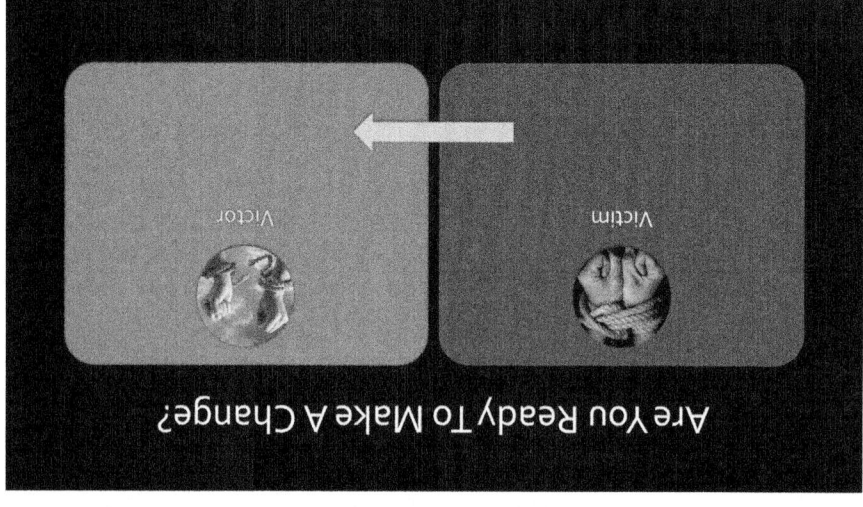

Are You Ready To Make A Change?

brought me to tears. In fact, at one point I had convinced myself that, that's what was needed to have a real breakthrough; the worse possible gut wrenching pain one could imagine and without it, you couldn't have a breakthrough. But that was not meant to be my journey. And it doesn't have to be yours.

My breakthrough was destined to come through my redundancy and a deep sense and desire to unlock my potential, to experience what it is like to live fully; to be the best version of me. No longer a victim but a victor; to make choices and firm decisions. When I realised that, and it took some time, I woke up and decided to live life at a higher level, to play hard, to love unconditionally, to embrace my failures, my pain, and problems knowing they were lessons that would inevitably make me stronger; mentally, physically, emotionally and spiritually. I asked better questions; what is the lesson here? How will this help me? What MUST I do?

Truth is, we get what we tolerate.

was in pain but I stuck a plaster over it, gritted my teeth and hoped for the best.

Having found a new job yet still feeling the constant bubbling and churning of discomfort inside my stomach, I considered the idea of going into business. It certainly woke me up and got me thinking creatively. And ever so slowly, as I gave time to letting my mind roam free into the unknown, the blinkers I had been wearing for years began to peel away and I could see glimmers of potential for a better life, not the hamster wheel I had been caught up on. I knew I had to move into a new way of being and that meant dealing with the stuff I had carefully placed the plaster over. From having to reconnect with my son, to walking away from the relationship I was in, I did what was required one painful task at a time. I took up running; it allowed me the freedom to literally cry out the pain that had been stripping my insides, whilst regaining my focus, helping me to let go of the tension that had gripped me so tightly at times I couldn't breathe.

Personal development and fitness became a way of life, my daily practice for positive living. And the more I committed to living a positive lifestyle, the more I felt in control and responsible for making life changing decisions. I became fearless in my attitude through facing my fears and placing my focus on creating the freedom I had been dreaming of.

Like you, I have heard other people's painful stories, journey's they had to go through to get to their breakthroughs and they have

If you woke up tomorrow and shouted out with meaning 'that's it, I revoke this life, I revoke this sense of not being enough, of not having enough, of having no control. I AM ENOUGH, I AM ABLE, I AM STRONG, I CAN DO THIS, I AM POWERFUL BEYOND MY CURRENT KNOWLEDGE and I AM COMMITTED TO BEGINNING MY JOURNEY', what do you think might happen? What might you begin to do differently? You see, we get bogged down with the 'how to' bring about change but believe me once you identify 'why' you want the change and make that ultimate decision to change, the how will appear.

Let me share with you what happens when you get to that stage. I found myself in a job where I loved the people I worked with, the company and the industry I was in but the role I had been promoted into turned out to be unfulfilling, unchallenging and lacking inspiration. What occurred out of that was complacency and acceptance; I knew I needed to change the situation but overall I thought I was happy. Then came the wake-up call; redundancy. I suddenly realised I was 38 with a 17-year old son I had not given enough attention to, exiting yet another broken relationship and going straight into another. Internally I was in a constant state of tension, butterflies, pounding headaches coming and going; completely out of sync with what I wanted. I felt vulnerable and at times sad, trying to ignore the external mess of my life which was a pure reflection of my inner turmoil. Outwardly, I held it together so no one knew what I was going through and how lost I felt. I

- You blame others, **externalise**

- You feel **out of control**

- You **hit rock bottom** – left with few friends, broken relationships, work issues due to lack of productivity, self-loathing

- You **think life is over** BUT you hang on in there desperate for change

Well, that change must be YOU!

Pain, Failure, and Fear

You've heard it all a million times and still, you are unhappy, unfulfilled, searching, lost, wondering when your time will come to be:

- Happy

- Fulfilled

- Loved

These things could be one turning point away… however, YOU must be willing to make the turn. The turn is in your hands. The change that is required lives inside your head; your mindset. The truth is our lives can change in one moment; with one choice, one decision.

- You think your **dreams are too big** and lofty so you bypass them – who the hell are you anyway?

- You are so **caught up in the rat race** you don't even realise life is passing you by – every day losing 24 hours of a limited lifespan. The only thing you know for certain is you will die

- You think **there is always tomorrow** – a lack of commitment to do anything today

- **Complacency** becomes your norm

- You are **trapped by the barrage of limiting beliefs** you are labelled with; from peers, parents, authoritarians, politicians, partners… you

- You get **depressed**, you **lose hope** for yourself

- You **hate the way you look** all the while being drip-fed media images of how you should look

- You **feel bad**, you **overeat**, **drink** more, **smoke** more, **moan** more

- You **bring other people down** with you because that makes you feel better

- **Life sucks** – or that's how you feel, anyway

- You search for solutions but fail to muster up the **energy** to see them through

CHAPTER 1
What's Wrong with Your Life?

Ask yourself; what's wrong with going through the motions of life? After all, everyone else appears to be doing it. In fact, your friends have jobs they aren't particularly happy with but they keep getting up at 7am to get to work by 9am to do the work they don't enjoy, to get home at 7pm to eat, moan and watch TV, to get the pay cheque that covers the bills (and for a few, pays for holidays) at the end of the month. If they are doing it, why shouldn't you? That's life.

But is it? Is that really, living? Are you allowing life to happen to you instead of you happening to life? Why would you do that? It could be for one or more of these reasons:

- You **make excuses** as to why you don't deserve better– **you're not enough**

- You feel **unappreciated,** even by your loved ones, reinforcing the 'not enough' myth

- You **'settle'** because, let's face it, others are doing less well than you so you should feel lucky

- You **undersell** yourself because you've been taught to; *'don't oversell yourself because life will disappoint you'*

- You **conform** because 'everyone else does', it is the norm

3

Finally, you acknowledge your current way of living doesn't fit. You want more but not what the media dictates to you as the things to strive for; the house, 2 cars, 2 kids and a family holiday per year, you want more because you feel you have more to offer. You know you have a purpose, you just don't know what it is.

Well, instead of ignoring the thought or putting it back on the shelf because 'you are so busy', deal with it. Enough excuses, enough tolerating, enough blaming; wake up and take the steps you need to, to be your best you. It is not feasible to complain about life if you are not willing to do something about it, to do something different.

And the truth is, you deserve to be your best you. Not only is it a chance to discover and explore your talents, skills, and interests, it is a journey that will help you identify why you are here and how YOU at your best can impact others…

INTRODUCTION
Life Sucks… Right?

You get to a certain point in life where you suddenly realise all is not as you would want it to be OR you feel so uncomfortable with life that you stop going through the motions just long enough to take stock.

This usually occurs when you are:

- Tired of feeling tired; dragging yourself from one task to another and through one day after another

- Bored with your life, knowing somewhere in your gut there are greater possibilities for you; you can do more

- Fed up with going through the motions, being in a zombie like state; what I call 'eyes wide shut'

- Tense and feeling the stress of life's pace, the constant challenges you face alone or feel you are facing alone

- Feeling you are missing out; like there is *a secret* someone forgot to share with you and that's why your life no longer satisfies you

- You feel unchallenged; you feel stuck in a cosy box of sameness and whilst that might be fine some days, most days it feels uncomfortable as if you are stunting your growth

Chance brought Yvonne and me together. Her recommendations were spot on and life changing. Yvonne is full of positive energy & genuine enthusiasm that cannot but rub off on everyone around her. She is extremely professional and focussed with a vision to empower as many people as possible to better their lives. I am sure she will achieve her goal; in fact, she is already doing it!"

Evi Kathrepti, Regional Trainer at Lifetime Training, Purpose Coach

Yvonne has a very calm yet reassuring manner and approach. It is a pleasure to work with someone with her kind yet containing energy. I hired Yvonne as a Coach and Mentor and she helped me to consider my business anew and reach new contacts to help me take my business to the next level.

Awele Odeh, MBACP, BSc(Hons)OT
Occupational Therapist & Trainer

"I'm delighted to recommend Yvonne as a first-class person to work with, be associated with and especially, to collaborate with. She is a born leader with a great sense of fun, a determination to only succeed and you know that when you collaborate with her, THE way will be found. It's a privilege to know her and work with her."

Wilma Allan, The Money Midwife
Speaker & Coach

"Yvonne is one of the most passionate people I've ever had the absolute pleasure to work with; very enthusiastic, authentic, energetic and highly knowledgeable. I consider her to be my first point of call for coaching and training. Her creativity, energy, and drive are inspiring, to say the least. She genuinely cares about the service she gives, the progress you make and the results you get. She doesn't let you slack; she supports you to be the best you can be because she believes in you and that kind of encouragement is priceless."

Michelle Margaret Marques, Founder & Creator
Elise Marques London

CLIENT TESTIMONIALS

"Yvonne is an extremely positive and inspiring individual. I, myself felt I had lost my way a little after a very draining life experience. I knew what I needed to do to get myself back on track and keep moving. Yvonne is a great listener and knew how to clarify my very disjointed story of myself of how I thought I had become lost. I found her to be very honest and straight to the point which always works for me."

Scarlett L. Christensen
Artist

"Yvonne is a rare person with amazing insight. She knows how to ask the right questions and she truly helped me understand myself better. I was impressed with every session by Yvonne's ability to help me discover solutions to problems in my personal and professional life. She is genuine and compassionate and incredibly optimistic. She always provided well thought out and constructive feedback and guidance. Yvonne took a personal interest in my life and I felt valued and motivated by her enthusiasm. I am honoured to have met this truly amazing woman."

Vickie Ellison
Fitness & Nutrition Coach

ACKNOWLEDGEMENT

As I sat down to write this page I was overwhelmed at the many people I wanted to thank, the many people who helped me along my road to self-discovery; a list that is continuously growing. But let me start with those who have been there every step of the way.

To my parents; you have truly been the wings beneath my feet. You have always had faith in your children and taught us the best lessons you had whilst allowing us to create our own. You gave us freedom to be who we are and that has been the greatest gift of all; thank you. And to my dearly departed dad, I love every memory you have left us with; we are blessed.

To my siblings; Joy, Errol, and Anne, you are my inspiration, my guiding light. Your support, love, and laughter continues to colour my life and will do forever.

To my son, Raphael, I love you to the moon and back. Having you taught me more about life, relationships and the meaning of unconditional love than any other lesson I have learned; and there have been many.

And to my extended family and friends whom I hold close to my heart, you are thanked for contributing to my life, for being a continuous blessing.

Table of Contents

Acknowledgement v

Introduction: Life Sucks… Right? 1

Chapter 1: What's Wrong with Your Life? 3

Chapter 2: There Comes a Turning Point 11

Chapter 3: Enter The 7F Principle 17

Chapter 4: Being Fit & Healthy 19

Chapter 5: Being Fearless 43

Chapter 6: Creating Freedom 53

Chapter 7: Family, Friends & Your Network 65

Chapter 8: Paying It Forward 79

Chapter 9: Having Fun 89

Chapter 10: Having Faith 97

Chapter 11: The Time for Change Is Now 105

About the Author 109

All Rights Reserved.

Copyright © Yvonne Bignall

No part of this book may be reproduced or transmitted in any form or by any means, electrical or mechanical, including photocopying and recording, or by any information storage or retrieval system without permission in writing from the author.

Disclaimer:

This book is written for informational purposes only. The author has made every effort to make sure the information is complete and accurate. All attempts have been made to verify information at the time of this publication and the author does not assume any responsibility for errors, omissions, or other interpretations of the subject matter.

The publisher and author shall have neither liability nor responsibility to any person or entity with respect to any loss or damage caused or alleged to be caused directly or indirectly by this book.

Suck It Up Or Change!

If you want a better life… YOU create it

Yvonne Bignall